ship

Lyndsey Winship is an arts journalist and film-maker who specialises in dance. A former dance editor at *Time Out*, she is currently dance critic of the *Evening Standard* and a regular contributor to the *Guardian*. A native of Newcastle, she now lives in north London.

Being a Dancer

Advice from Dancers and Choreographers

Lyndsey Winship

NICK HERN BOOKS

London

www.nickhernbooks.co.uk

A Nick Hern Book

BEING A DANCER

First published in Great Britain in 2015
by Nick Hern Books Limited
The Glasshouse, 49a Goldhawk Road, London W12 8QP

Copyright © 2015 Lyndsey Winship

Lyndsey Winship has asserted her right
to be identified as the author of this work

Cover image: Carlos Acosta, 2011
© Johan Persson/ArenaPAL

Designed and typeset by
Nick Hern Books, London
Printed and bound in Great Britain by
Ashford Colour Press, Gosport, Hampshire

A CIP catalogue record for this book
is available from the British Library

ISBN 978 1 84842 462 3

Contents

CONTENTS

Introduction

You have to love dancing to stick to it. It gives you nothing back, no manuscripts to store away, no paintings to show on walls and maybe hang in museums, no poems to be printed and sold, nothing but that single fleeting moment when you feel alive. **Merce Cunningham**

Dancers are extraordinary creatures. They endure pain, rejection, injury, years of intensive training, against-the-odds competition, poor salaries and cruelly short careers. Yet in more than a decade of writing about dance, I've never met a dancer who didn't think they had the best job in the world.

As a performer, dance offers a fusion of the physical, the intellectual, the creative and even the spiritual, in a way that's hard to find anywhere else. It's an incredible career, but it's also an incredibly tough one, and many budding dancers never quite realise their full potential.

It's an art form that's passed on from dancer to dancer, generation to generation – the physical equivalent of an oral tradition. But while the steps are passed down, the practicalities of making a career in dance might not be. Where and when should you train? How do you get a job with a dance company? How can you protect your body from injury? How do you become a choreographer?

This book attempts to uncover answers to those questions, drawing on the wisdom of those who've been there and done it. There is advice from some of the best dancers in the world, crossing the fields of ballet, contemporary, South Asian dance and hip hop, and covering subjects both motivational and mundane, from tapping into your own reserves of creativity and resilience, to the important question of when to eat your pre-show banana.

The dancers in these pages have performed with the likes of the Royal Ballet, English National Ballet, Rambert, Matthew Bourne's New Adventures and BalletBoyz; they are stars of the West End stage, TV talent-show successes and Kylie's backing dancers – as well as some of Britain's leading choreographers.

Dancers are used to speaking with their bodies, but are less often asked to voice their opinions. Yet, as you'll see, they have plenty to say. And despite being an intensely competitive world – although *nothing* like *Black Swan*, as more than one interviewee was keen to point out – a group of warmer, more enthusiastic and supportive artists it would be hard to find. 'Never trust an expert,' says choreographer Wayne McGregor, but there's plenty of expert advice here that's worth listening to, whether practical encouragement or tough love. And these experts are not always in agreement.

This book is designed to be dipped into at leisure or read straight through, and within it you will find advice for dancers at every stage of their career, whether that's a ballet bunhead dreaming of *Swan Lake*, a b-boy wanting to hone his skills, a new graduate looking for a job or a professional dancer trying to up their game. Whether you are an aspiring choreographer or company director, or just a dance fan interested in the workings of a dancer's life – and perhaps looking to be inspired by some of the hardest grafting people in the arts – there is something here for you.

And be sure, the end result of all that hard work is worth it. As American dancer Agnes de Mille said: 'When you perform... you are out of yourself – larger and more potent, more beautiful. You are for minutes heroic. This is power. This is glory on earth. And it is yours, nightly.' When the muscles are aching, just keep that one in mind.

Lyndsey Winship

The Dancers
and Choreographers

Carlos Acosta
Born in Cuba, Acosta danced with English National Ballet and Houston Ballet before joining the Royal Ballet in 1998. One of the biggest ballet stars of today, idolised around the world, Acosta is famous for his virtuosic technique and magnetic charisma.

Matthew Bourne
Britain's most popular contemporary choreographer made his name with his all-male version of *Swan Lake* in 1995, which he has followed with witty, modern takes on other classic stories, including *Sleeping Beauty*, *The Nutcracker* and *The Car Man* [*Carmen*] for his company New Adventures.

Teneisha Bonner
A leading hip-hop performer, Bonner's career spans both the theatre and commercial worlds. She has starred in the shows *Some Like It Hip Hop* and *Into the Hoods*, and performed with the likes of Kylie Minogue and Take That, as well as appearing in the film *StreetDance 3D*.

Darcey Bussell
Britain's best-known ballerina since Margot Fonteyn, Bussell became a principal dancer at the Royal Ballet aged twenty, plucked out of the corps de ballet by choreographer Kenneth MacMillan, who created leading

roles for her in the ballets *The Prince of the Pagodas* and *Winter Dreams*. She is now president of the Royal Academy of Dance, a television presenter and judge on *Strictly Come Dancing*.

Lauren Cuthbertson
The top British ballerina of her generation, Cuthbertson is a principal dancer at the Royal Ballet, known for her warm and natural character on stage. She created the lead role of Alice in Christopher Wheeldon's *Alice's Adventures in Wonderland*.

Maxine Doyle
Choreographer and director Doyle is Associate Director of immersive theatre company Punchdrunk, masterminding productions including *Sleep No More*, *Masque of the Red Death* and *The Drowned Man*.

Tommy Franzén
Born in Sweden, Tommy Franzén is a versatile performer working in hip hop (*Some Like It Hip Hop, The Five & the Prophecy of Prana*), contemporary (Russell Maliphant Company), ballet (*Goldberg*) and in film (*Mamma Mia! The Movie*). He was the runner-up in TV dance competition *So You Think You Can Dance?*

Adam Garcia
Dancer and actor who came to prominence in the show *Tap Dogs* and went on to take the lead role in *Saturday Night Fever*. Garcia starred in the 2000 film *Coyote Ugly*, and was on the judging panel of TV talent show *Got to Dance*.

Jonathan Goddard
Twice winner of Best Male Dancer at the National Dance Awards, Goddard is a contemporary dancer of rare

eloquence, grace and style. After performing with Richard Alston Dance Company and Rambert, he now pursues a freelance career. He is part of New Movement Collective and was acclaimed for his performance as the titular lead in Mark Bruce's *Dracula*.

Matthew Golding

Born in Saskatchewan, Canada, Golding dreamed of being a professional ice-hockey player before injury made him change track. A performer with the princely bearing of a classic *danseur noble*, he danced with American Ballet Theatre and Dutch National Ballet before becoming a principal dancer with the Royal Ballet.

Melissa Hamilton

Hailing from Northern Ireland, Hamilton trained at Elmhurst School for Dance and then privately with Masha Mukhamedov in Athens before winning the Youth America Grand Prix and joining the Royal Ballet in 2007.

Wayne McGregor

The first contemporary choreographer to become resident choreographer at the Royal Ballet, McGregor founded his own company, Wayne McGregor | Random Dance, in 1992, and is known for his endless curiosity and hyper-kinetic choreography that pushes the body to extremes. McGregor is an inveterate collaborator and has worked with an eclectic range of artists, musicians, writers and scientists.

Steven McRae

Australian McRae is a principal dancer with the Royal Ballet. A dancer of great speed, precision and power, he excels in virtuoso roles.

Stephen Mear

Leading musical-theatre choreographer whose credits include *Gypsy, Mary Poppins, Singin' in the Rain, Anything Goes, The Little Mermaid, Crazy for You* and *Acorn Antiques.*

Cassa Pancho

Founder and Artistic Director of Ballet Black, a company of black and Asian dancers. Pancho also runs the Ballet Black school in west London.

Seeta Patel

Independent dance artist and choreographer working in Bharata Natyam and contemporary dance. Her works include *First Light, Unspoken Voices, Dancing My Siva* and the film *The Art of Defining Me*, with co-creator Kamala Devam.

Arlene Phillips

Choreographer and director who founded the dance troupe Hot Gossip in 1974 and went on to have a varied career, working across film, television, musical theatre, advertising and music videos.

Arthur Pita

A former dancer with Matthew Bourne's New Adventures, Pita now works as a choreographer across theatre, opera and film, making work for adults and children. He won a South Bank Sky Arts Award for *The Metamorphosis.*

Kate Prince

Founder of ZooNation, the UK's leading hip-hop dance company, choreographer Prince is responsible for the acclaimed shows *Into the Hoods* and *Some Like It Hip Hop.* She also runs the ZooNation Youth Company and the ZooNation Academy of Dance.

Matthew Rees

Rees learned to dance at school and has no other formal training. He was planning to join the Marines before he was given the opportunity to work with the original BalletBoyz, Michael Nunn and William Trevitt, becoming a founder member of BalletBoyz – The Talent in 2010.

Tamara Rojo

Born in Spain, Rojo is one of the world's leading ballet dancers. As a member of the Royal Ballet between 2000 and 2012, she became known for her depth of dramatic expression. Rojo now combines a dancing career with her role as Artistic Director of English National Ballet.

Kenrick 'H2O' Sandy

Sandy founded the hip-hop company Boy Blue Entertainment in 2002 and scored a major hit with *Pied Piper*, for which the company won an Olivier Award. He also choreographs for pop acts including Rita Ora and Dizzee Rascal, and worked on the 2012 London Olympic Opening Ceremony.

Hofesh Shechter

London-based Israeli choreographer known for his earthy style and atmospheric productions. Shechter first grabbed the audience's attention with his all-male piece *Uprising* in 2006, and had his biggest success with the guitar-fuelled *Political Mother* in 2010.

Aaron Sillis

Dancer and choreographer in contemporary and commercial dance. Theatre credits include *The Most Incredible Thing*, *Matthew Bourne's Dorian Gray*, *Movin' Out*. He has performed with Kylie Minogue, Rihanna and Katy Perry among others, and now choreographs for FKA twigs.

Marlon 'Swoosh' Wallen
Dancer and Artistic Director of Flawless, the street-dance crew who got to the finals of *Britain's Got Talent* in 2009, and have since created their own national tour and collaborated with English National Ballet.

1
Training

Why Dance?

In this book, you'll hear all the ways in which dance is one of the toughest careers out there. So if that's the case, why on earth would you want to do it?

I think without doubt it's the best job in the world. Using your physicality, your moving body, as a way of lifting the spirit; that buzz of exhilaration and inspiration, being able to express yourself. And creating a bit of magic, transporting people out of their everyday world. It's a lovely escape. **Darcey Bussell**

I remember my very first lesson. I was always that child who hid behind my mum's leg. I don't think of myself as shy, but I guess I was. But I can remember that first lesson spinning and jumping as high as I could. Suddenly I felt free. **Steven McRae**

As a child, I thought it was a magical career, where your spirit marries with your body to create this artistry, to achieve moments of connection with the audience. And it is like that. I remember that feeling of standing in the wings and feeling revved up, going to attack the stage, and that wonderful, amazing feeling that you can open your soul and share it with the audience. **Arthur Pita**

The best thing about working in dance is working with dancers. Dancers are amazing; they are generous, egoless, brilliant people. The best thing is being able to go to work and be inspired every day. It's a privilege. **Maxine Doyle**

It's the performing that makes it worthwhile. The minute that curtain goes up. Some days your body says no, or things happen that are out of your control – maybe the conductor doesn't play your preferred tempo, or your costume got altered wrong. But there are random and rare occasions when you feel like something clicks, and it can last ten seconds or it can last a whole act, and when those moments happen it is incredible. I've been fortunate to feel that a few times. I think every dancer searches for that every time they go on stage. **Steven McRae**

Starting Out

If you want to be a professional dancer, does it matter at what age you start to train? If you didn't don a tutu aged three, is it too late to achieve your dreams? Some say yes, others disagree. Some say natural talent can push through at any age, others that you need to put in your ten thousand hours. Unlike in many careers, dancers normally decide on their vocation at a very early age, but there are always exceptions.

I can think of a million examples of people who started when they were six and people who started when they were eighteen. I've always danced all my life, but I didn't train properly till I was twenty-five. There are many ways. **Kate Prince**

As a girl, for classical ballet, the age you start really matters. In my ballet school we take them at three, but you start to see what a child is really capable of by six or seven. Cira Robinson [of Ballet Black] started at eight or nine and she did very well, and we had another great dancer who started at fourteen, but she had years of gymnastics under her belt. Guys can get away with starting later, which is a bit unfair. **Cassa Pancho**

I started really young, at three, jumping around, pretending to be a kite. I had a couple of years, aged four or five where I gave up – you know, the wilderness period – then I carried on. What was good about being that young and just doing free movement is that I wasn't influenced by anything. **Jonathan Goddard**

I went to college at sixteen as a good street dancer with no training. I wanted to be a pop star. But through learning all the different dance forms I really got into contemporary. I loved the discipline of ballet, I found a love for all these different dance styles. I think sixteen's a great age to go. **Aaron Sillis**

If you want to make a profession of it, then, in theory, no later than thirteen is probably a gauge. I know boys who've started later than that, but that's when they're sporty and flexible and strong. **Darcey Bussell**

I started at the age of three, but I don't think it matters. Ultimately good training is what matters. The hardest thing to correct in a dancer is bad habits. Try to get into the best training you can, early on. **Lauren Cuthbertson**

In Cuba, I started break-dancing in the eighties. I was imitating Michael Jackson and so my father forced me into ballet. He grabbed me by the hand and said, 'This is what you're going to do.' For three years I struggled. I had the ability to mimic movement very well, but I was unreliable. They cast me in shows and didn't know if I was going to turn up or not. One time they had to stop a show for an hour and a half to look for me. I was out playing, they found me completely soaked in mud. At the age of thirteen I saw the National Ballet of Cuba for the first time. That's when I fell in love with it. I saw the professionals doing all the lifts and carrying the girl with one hand and I decided, 'I want to do that.' **Carlos Acosta**

I went to the Jerusalem Academy for Dance and Music at fifteen and that was the first time I did serious dance – up until then I did folk dance. I was pretty horrific at the beginning, I couldn't dance. But after a couple of years I think I made a lot of progress. A choreographer came to work with us who really helped me. I think she recognised that I did the best with what I have. I was giving my all, really putting myself into it. **Hofesh Shechter**

I started at eighteen. I was not into dancing before that, I was into sport and art. The first routine I learnt was from an eleven-year-old. I thought, 'Maybe I'm a bit too old to start here.' But I don't think there's any age restriction. Some people say the younger the better, but I don't think that matters. It's about the confidence that person has. **Kenrick Sandy**

I was a self-taught dancer. When I was four I was copying Michael Jackson and James Brown and Gene Kelly. I'd been freestyling, doing my own street-dance moves. I had no idea what I was doing until I got to college and took a BTEC National dance course. That's what opened my mind to ballet, contemporary, jazz, and that took me to another level to be a better dancer. **Marlon Wallen**

I didn't start dancing till I was twelve, because of an amazing secondary schoolteacher who had a dance club at school. I discovered a passion to move, but I also knew from an early age that I was never going to be an amazing dancer and that was fine, because I was more interested in being in control. As soon as I started dancing, I started choreographing. **Maxine Doyle**

I don't think it really matters what age you start. The last show I did, some people had danced for three years, some people for over twenty years, and we were all doing the same show. I was just turning eleven when I started street dance classes. It was just fun and it ignited my fire for dance, so it really worked for me. **Tommy Franzén**

Martha Graham started when she was twenty-six. It should come to you when you're ready. For me, I was eight, and it was because I saw John Travolta and I just wanted to do what he did. **Arthur Pita**

I will always vouch for a classical training, but it's also the most boring way to start when you're little. I started at ten, which in dance terms is quite late, but I'm glad because it was my choice to do it, not my parents'. Of the students who trained with me, I'm one of the few people that has continued as a professional dancer and I think that's partly because my parents were really hands-off. It helps to find an autonomy and a desire to do it on your own. **Seeta Patel**

If you believe the theory that you need ten thousand hours of practice to become good at anything then, yes, the sooner you start the better. But in ballet there is also a level of natural talent. The more talent you have the less practice you need sometimes. **Tamara Rojo**

I like the idea that people don't get into training too early. I like dancers who've got other interests, who've seen other things, experienced life a bit more, rather than that dedicated dance training, moving from one institution to another. I like the idea of people starting at sixteen, maybe seventeen or eighteen. I wouldn't recommend it quite so late as me – twenty-two – but I was sort of self-taught before that. **Matthew Bourne**

I don't think I'd still have this passion for dance if I'd started very young. I started at the Brit School at sixteen, but I always used to dance around on my own. At secondary school I would ask the teacher for the drama-room key and go in there and dance around by myself. At college my path was constantly crossed by people who'd been doing it since they were sperms, with pushy parents. They'd kind of forgotten why they were doing it. They had burnt out. And there was me all excited. **Teneisha Bonner**

At the National Ballet School in Canada, when I didn't get a scholarship they said, 'If he doesn't come now it's too late.' My parents couldn't afford it and the school said, 'He'll have no dance career.' But I kept dancing and at fourteen I went to ballet school and it wasn't too late. Everyone develops at different ages. **Matthew Golding**

I didn't start till I was sixteen. If you've got a natural 'something', it doesn't matter what age you start, it just takes a certain amount of time to develop. I ended up taking Dance for GCSE then A level. I auditioned for The Place, but it was really expensive to go, so at eighteen I decided to apply for the Marines and got a job at River Island while getting my fitness up. There was an audition for BalletBoyz – The Talent and I just went for it, not thinking I'd have a hope in hell, but I got it. That put a spanner in the works. **Matthew Rees**

What School? What Style?

If you want to be a dancer, is it imperative to go to a full-time dance school? How do you get in? (And what if you don't?) The buzzword these days is diversity — and we're not talking about the street-dance crew — so what about different dance styles? As boundaries between genres blur, dancers are expected to be able to switch from one style to another in quick succession. Our dancers talk about the value of a broad dance education and a great teacher, and why, even if you're a b-boy, perhaps you should learn ballet as well.

I think dance schools are looking for raw potential, I don't think they're looking for a finished product. It's a canvas that they can work on. **Lauren Cuthbertson**

I hadn't done a dance class prior to going to the Brit School, but I did gymnastics and I had a natural knack for dance. I was fortunate – my pointed foot was pretty much a flex at the time, but they saw that there was potential. **Teneisha Bonner**

To get into dance school you need to do your research. Look at all the schools and their past students and see if there are people you recognise that have been through that system. You also need to be realistic about what you've got to offer. You need some outside advice about what your strengths are to find the right school for you. **Aaron Sillis**

I should have it tattooed on my forehead that the Royal Ballet School is not the only school. Many great dancers did not go there. We've had a lot of kids come to us saying, 'I didn't get into the Royal Ballet School, my dance career is over.' And we say, hang on, there are other schools, there are other places, other countries. **Cassa Pancho**

I did ballet as a hobby till I was sixteen, one day a week after school. But then I got it into my head that I wanted a career in ballet. I wasn't accepted in the Royal Ballet School. I ended up going to Elmhurst and I was told I had the wrong body after my first year, that I was totally unsuitable for ballet. It left me distraught, my dreams shattered. Then I left and trained privately for ten months in Athens. At eighteen, I did an audition class for the Royal Ballet and got my contract on the spot. It wasn't self-belief, it was a desire to prove people wrong. People told me I couldn't do it so I was like, 'I will find a way.' **Melissa Hamilton**

There are many different routes to becoming a dancer and they don't all have to be conventional. So if you get a knock-back, if you don't get into the school that you wanted to go to, or the path to being a dancer seems obstructed – which is what happened to me – find another way. **Kate Prince**

We don't audition people who haven't done a proper formal training of at least three years at one of the recognised dance colleges. **Matthew Bourne**

I used to think going to vocational dance school was more important, but now I'm encountering people that trained in Shaolin kung fu and rhythmic gymnastics. The titans of modern dance techniques – Cunningham and Graham – are starting to slide away. Ballet is fairly constant. I think whatever your practice you should touch base with ballet. Don't be scared of it. If you're scared of it you've got the wrong teacher. **Jonathan Goddard**

There are so many syllabuses. Cecchetti is an incredibly strong syllabus for classical ballet, for a professional, in the long term it really sets you up. RAD has a very good basis to start you off. But it's often really down to the teacher, not just the syllabus. Get recommendations, and don't get stuck with one teacher. I did a lot of outside classes which really opened my mind. **Darcey Bussell**

One of the things that's really helped in my seventeen-year career is diversity. I don't want to pigeonhole myself. To broaden my scope of working with different choreographers I've had to be a chameleon. I would have cut off a lot of opportunities and relationships if I hadn't approached dance like that. **Teneisha Bonner**

Experience as many dance styles as possible. Try them all. You might have an idea of one style of dance that's inspired you, but don't limit yourself to that. **Darcey Bussell**

It doesn't matter how you start. I did social dance – ballroom and Latin American and disco. That was my training. **Wayne McGregor**

I started off with freestyle disco dancing. I loved the freedom. It was just moving to music and rhythm and getting that into your body. It wasn't very technical, but I think it was a good start. When I got to high school we did ballet, contemporary, Greek dancing and flamenco. It was a fantastic combination. Flamenco taught you about rhythm, power and attack, and playing your body like an instrument. And ballet is the bible. You can't not have it. **Arthur Pita**

I did jazz, that's how I got good at turning and picking up steps. Tap is good for musicality and understanding how you can play with phrasing. When I came to ballet school I thought, 'This is very slow and hard and tedious.' It's good to do modern classes, some free dancing to change it up. **Matthew Golding**

For a classical dancer it's incredibly important to do contemporary, because it will only assist your classical dance. **Darcey Bussell**

I think the demands on dancers are much greater than ever. At one time dancers weren't expected to do so many different styles. When I was first teaching in London I used to get a lot of the Royal Ballet dancers coming to my rock-jazz classes in secret. Nowadays the classical dancers are exploring all kinds of contemporary dance and the dancers are being pushed beyond the limits, not just of the body but of the mind. **Arlene Phillips**

Become versatile. So that whatever movement style you meet you're able to adapt. So that you're able to do more with your body, with your energy. I was never great at ballet, but I appreciate that it gives me something, strength, a way of looking at the body and aligning it, a richness. There are a lot of dancers out there and a lot of competition, so the more you keep your options open, the better. **Hofesh Shechter**

The thing I say most often to the boys at our school is that they need to become more diverse and they need to learn ballet and technique and gymnastics and work on their agility. For girls, in the hip-hop/commercial industry, I say learn how to dance on the floor, do a bit of breaking, learn a trick. And don't rely on just being sexy, because that's boring. **Kate Prince**

I took myself off to ballet when I was fifteen at my local school to get some more technique. The teacher said, 'You can come to do ballet, but you have to start at the bottom,' so I was in the class with the six-year-olds, which was funny. I didn't really care. It was all part of the process of training. I knew that it was important to train as much as I could. **Maxine Doyle**

In musical theatre, dancers need to have a basic technique, a strong ballet technique. I remember hating it at first, but it taught me how to do pirouettes, how to spot, how to turn. It's basic training: find your centre. And it's great for your posture. **Stephen Mear**

In musical theatre, it happens time and time again that you get the most phenomenal dancers and then the musical director will say, 'Sorry, you've got a "D" voice and we can't put you on a mic.' Dancers who want to do musical theatre have to remember the big picture, they have to be able to sing and they have to work on it equally as hard as they do their dancing. **Arlene Phillips**

Going to stage school, doing ballet and contemporary, that's a much more institutionalised kind of schooling. From a hip-hop/street-dance perspective you have to live it, be going to classes, going to battles, going to the underground events. That's a different kind of schooling, that's a cultural kind of schooling. **Kenrick Sandy**

I used to teach six or seven days a week all over London, save my money, and then go out to New York, LA or Paris with all my savings, for a week at a time, to do class every day. It's great. It throws you in at the deep end and you learn from lots of people. **Kate Prince**

I did a degree in Dance and English, then I applied for an MA, and in the interim I just did everything I could, loads of independent training, loads of classes and workshops. Not just dance, but writing courses and poetry courses and seeing lots of art. I remember reading something Martha Graham said about educating yourself as an artist constantly. And I remember reading somewhere that Pina Bausch used to listen to eight hours of classical music a day. Everything informs you as a theatre-maker. **Maxine Doyle**

My first obstacle was how to combine academic education with ballet practice and I was very lucky because my mother wouldn't compromise. Unless I finished my studies I was not allowed to dance, and I will be forever grateful to her for that. It always concerns me to see that some dance schools think that's not important. A ballet career can be very, very short and you need to ensure you have a safety net, and your academic schooling is one of those safety nets. **Tamara Rojo**

Learning a classical art form can be boring to start off with. You can't always find the excitement, but hopefully a teacher will be able to give it to you. **Seeta Patel**

I did the Royal Ballet Junior Associate programme at eight and the summer school – which is quite intense when you're nine or ten years old. I didn't enjoy all of it. I found Junior Associates so boring. For me, the brutal training of dance rained on my imaginative parade. And so I would be naughty and rebel and then get told off. The freedom I had in my old ballet school to be able to just dance around is what kept me going. **Lauren Cuthbertson**

My very first teacher taught me to be fearless, to turn faster, jump higher. 'You can jump higher than that!' she would say. 'Why can't you do the splits?' So I would stretch every day until I could do the splits. There was never any question, it was, 'Just do it.' I remember aged eight she was teaching me double *tours en l'air*. I just threw myself around. A lot of dancers lose that freedom. **Steven McRae**

My teacher picked me out and there was an instant trust, instant belief, a connection. It's important for you to be listened to. With a teacher, if you don't trust that person, it won't work. I've seen dancers work with certain people and get worse. It's so important for a dancer to have a good coach. **Melissa Hamilton**

I was never top of the class, the teacher's pet. I had a lot of ups and downs, but I had teachers that held on to me and said, 'I believe in you. Let's give it another go.' **Matthew Golding**

I was told by teachers that I would never be a dancer, but I knew that dancing was what I wanted to make my life. I went to university and I was dancing with other like-minded, self-taught people. No, I didn't go to a well-known college, but I got a lot of hands-on experience. Don't let someone tell you that you can't, there's always a way. You might not be the prima ballerina – you might end up being a dance teacher or a choreographer – but you can still make dance your life if that's what you're passionate about. **Kate Prince**

Getting Better:
Improving Technique

*We all want to be the kind of dancer who can make jaws drop,
with a giant leap, virtuosic turns or a trick that no one has seen
before. But all those moves begin in the studio, with days, weeks,
years of practice. How do you become a better dancer? How can
you push your technique to the highest level? And are there any
short cuts?*

Class for me is the most vital tool. That hour and fifteen
each day is my daily vitamin, it's like giving my body a
grease and oil change. For me, class is technique, technique,
technique. It's like building blocks. You just have to keep
on adding them and adding them. The minute you walk in
and you don't push the technique, you're only going to fall
backwards. It takes years and years to build your technique,
but it can go so quickly. **Steven McRae**

It's about putting the hours in. It's about drilling technique, particularly when it comes to turns and jumps.
You've got to keep going and keep going until it becomes
familiar. **Kate Prince**

A lot of it is just working and working, because repetition creates instinct, especially in ballet. It is literally
repeating things so many times that it becomes muscle
memory. Only now when I'm about to stop dancing do
I feel like I am a good dancer, for the first time in my life.
Now my body knows how to do things, it's not my mind

telling me how to do it, it's my body. That's just repetition until your body can do it without you having to dedicate the attention to it. **Tamara Rojo**

You have to know the strengths and weaknesses in your physique. Am I a good jumper, or a good turner? How am I in adagio? It's not just playing to your strengths, but working on your weaknesses as well. **Darcey Bussell**

You have to do additional work on your own. If your leg doesn't go high enough, you need to do something about it. Don't wait for it to get up there – it's not going to do that. Identify the problem and ask for help. Get to class an hour early and get your leg on the barre and stretch it, or do strengthening exercises. There's a dangerous culture of waiting for people to make you good, to make you perform better. You have to do it yourself. **Cassa Pancho**

You see something and think, 'Wow, that's impossible,' but you have to learn to break it down. You do complementary exercises to get you there. You strengthen your muscles for the landing, you work on the *ballon*, the *relevé*. It's slow-burn, but it's persisting every day until your brain and muscle memory are getting that information. **Carlos Acosta**

To improve, it's thinking about things that will help you get to the end result, and not just trying to do the end result. If you want to be able to do a massive split *jeté* and you can't do the splits yet, it's not going to happen. So you have to work on your stretching and strength and flexibility and work on your jumps and bit by bit you'll find that the two will marry. **Lauren Cuthbertson**

It all boils down to training. We have particular drills that we teach. Those drills can be very tiring, very boring, but it forms your body to be able to do the flashy stuff. If you want to have some impressive flips and tricks, you have to go through the gymnastic drills, from the forward rolls to the cartwheels, to the roundoffs, and that's the same procedure. Build up to it. **Marlon Wallen**

It's about going over the same move over and over again. I may work on a cartwheel for three weeks but I'll be looking at how many different versions of a cartwheel I can do. Two-handed, one-handed, one-handed with the following hand, no hands, cartwheel on the forearm. You perfect each of them to the level where it becomes like water, so when I do a move it just flows. **Kenrick Sandy**

In school you're a little soldier. It's not military, but it's all discipline. **Matthew Golding**

Take class with everyone and absorb as much as you can. Try to make your way into companies and take class. I was very good at that. I remember in Paris, waiting around to see dancers coming through the stage door and just joining them and doing class with Paris Opera Ballet aged eighteen for a whole week without anyone asking any questions. Gatecrash as much as you can! **Tamara Rojo**

You need to focus on what the teachers are saying, and be observant of what's going on around you. I like really paying attention to other dancers to see what I can take from them. We get so focused on looking in the mirror, it's really important to step back a bit and observe other people's talents, you can learn so much. **Aaron Sillis**

I looked at all the people I worked with who were really great dancers – like Dein Perry, who created *Tap Dogs* – and I loved the way they moved, so I'd just copy them. Simple as that: pure thieving plagiarism. Absorb all the people around you, how they move, what they do in the rehearsal room. Dancers learn by imitation. **Adam Garcia**

The only way you learn to pick up steps quickly is practice. Take fast classes, where they demonstrate the exercises quickly. You have to go through that process of thinking, 'It's too fast. I don't understand what's going on!' Find someone in the class who does know what they're doing and learn it from them. Through time it will speed up how fast you can pick up an exercise. **Jonathan Goddard**

My attitude towards technique has changed. In the past few years I've started to work a lot smarter. When I was younger it was just work, the amount of it. Now I think you have to constantly face up to your weaknesses. You can't cheat. You can't rely on what is already there. **Melissa Hamilton**

I think an important thing, if you look at a lot of the dancers that are at the top, is that there's an intelligence. They obviously have gifts, but they have the intelligence to exploit those gifts. It's not about repeating something till you're blue in the face. It's about listening to what your body needs, what perhaps a coach has suggested, what the role needs, as opposed to just repeating it ten times badly. **Steven McRae**

I have a sports scientist to help me target specific things, at 8.30 a.m. for an hour every day. If I'm doing one ballet that needs jumps, I will target jumps a few months before. If I want to work on my flexibility, I do that. Because I know I don't have the hours in the day to just rehearse until I get it. **Tamara Rojo**

I constantly tell my students to be present and project, and be muscular. It sounds weird to think that people dance without being muscular, but you can dance in a way that isn't really physically invested and that's what I'm always frustrated by. Think about what is happening in the body. Don't just move the arm in a circle, think about where it's coming from and what it connects to. **Seeta Patel**

You learn a lot by teaching. You can learn a move even better by teaching it. And together we progress quicker than if everyone was to hold on to their moves and work on their own things. **Tommy Franzén**

People say, 'You're the one with no training!' When I joined BalletBoyz it was difficult and I remember struggling quite a bit with ballet. I think there are some video clips of me sneaking around in the background pretending I know what I'm doing. It just snapped one day, I thought to myself, 'Sort it out, go in there and think you're the dog's...' and it seemed to work. Convince yourself that you can do this, and it slowly works. **Matthew Rees**

When I was in my home town I was the best there, and I got to college, London Studio Centre, and I was probably one of the worst, technically. I was in the lowest ballet class, and I was determined before I left that I would be in the top. I made myself do fourteen ballet classes a week. I worked on things I was weakest on. And I got there, by the skin of my teeth. It's easy to do the classes you're good at. Push yourself at the things you're not good at. **Stephen Mear**

At school we would always practise our *fouettés* on Sundays when everyone else was at home. We'd go into a studio and try to get up to forty-eight. You'd be dizzy and falling everywhere, but you'd keep going. Make it into a game and mess around and do fun things. And then in class it's important that you really discipline yourself and fine-tune that into something that's a bit more refined. **Lauren Cuthbertson**

In Cuba there's an atmosphere of collectivity, of wanting to practise together. It's 'Let's compete!' and 'How many pirouettes can you do?' and then it's girls against boys to see how many turns they can do. Ballet is cool there. It's not you, the individual, it's collectivity. Everybody's doing it and you want to do it too, you've got this mass vibe. **Carlos Acosta**

For tap dancing, learn to jam. You're not a tap dancer unless you can make music yourself and be at home with your feet. I did a show with Baz Luhrmann at Sydney Festival. I was one of two tap-dancing bellboys. We had to stand outside and dance as the crowd came in. My partner said, 'We're just going to trade eights.' I was like, 'What?' I was terrible for the first night, and then I couldn't look like a dickhead so I had to learn. It's about play, knowing small portions of steps and then just going for it. **Adam Garcia**

I'm not a freestyle dancer, but it's a skill you need in the commercial hip-hop world. To get better, just do it more often. You can dance around in your room. You could go to a club where dancers go and everyone's freestyling. Go somewhere where no one knows you. Put sunglasses on so no one can recognise you. Just have a good time. **Tommy Franzén**

Be open to going at the problem in a new way. When I was learning to do alphas – that's a move where you jump on two hands and both legs come off the floor – I just couldn't get them. It turned out all I needed was a bit of pressure. When I was in front of the audience, I'd be able to do it. Any other time I couldn't. I thought, the more times I do it badly, the more that's what my muscles are remembering. So I wouldn't practise at all. I'd get on stage, do one good one, once a day, and then when I came back from tour I could do them. **Teneisha Bonner**

Usually if you're trying to get a step, letting go is the best way of getting it. The more you fight it, it's not going to happen. The best way to improve is to let go. **Matthew Golding**

Dealing with Bullies

Although the image of boys who dance has transformed since the all-conquering Billy Elliot and the ever-growing popularity of street dance, teasing and bullying still does affect some young male dancers. Rise above it, say our pros.

I used to dance in school plays, I was the only boy in *Grease*, I danced to Madonna's 'Holiday' with six girls and I got bullied by all the guys. Now I've been a dancer for Madonna. I was on set with Kylie recently where she was playing a Sleeping Beauty and I was her Prince Charming and had to give her the kiss of life. I said to Kylie, 'When I was fourteen I sang one of your songs and got bullied for it.' And she burst out laughing and said, 'Ha, look at you now! You're giving me the kiss of life. Take that, haters!' **Aaron Sillis**

I was called twinkletoes on the football pitch; I would point my toes in basketball when I was going for jump shots, which caused people entertainment, but it was all lighthearted. I went to an all-boys' school and said to one guy, 'So while you're hugging other boys playing rugby, I get to look at girls in leotards all Saturday.' He was like, 'Oh. Dammit.' It disarmed him, in a way. **Adam Garcia**

I remember being teased at school. But in my little town, all the teenage girls went to the disco-dancing school. So when I went to high school they were the popular girls and I was the mascot. All the big, cool, bully guys were into those girls so I had this protection. It's hard not to be scarred by teasing. The advice would be, just block it out, be above it. And make friends with the popular girls – they will protect you! **Arthur Pita**

Are You Hungry Enough?

How much do you want it? Just enjoying dance isn't enough to make it into your career. You have to need it more than anything else, say the dancers who've been there. When it takes this much hard work, only the most passionate will make it.

The most important thing is you have to know that you can't live without dancing – just wanting it isn't good enough. It has to be like breathing. I need to dance to breathe. There are so many people wanting to dance, wanting to make careers in dance, you just can't think, 'Ooh, that would be nice.' It isn't going to work. **Arlene Phillips**

Only do it if you're consumed by it. I remember Felix [Barrett, Punchdrunk's Artistic Director] said to me once, 'Maxine, what else would we do?' We wouldn't be able to do anything else. I envy people who do other things well. **Maxine Doyle**

You need to have drive, otherwise you won't make it in the ballet world. There has to be something that makes you want to get up in the morning and do what we do, because it's not normal. I would love to do an experiment with dancers and find out if there's something common in their psyche that makes them want to do it. It's so masochistic. **Melissa Hamilton**

Are there myths about being a dancer? Yes, that it's all glamour. It isn't glamorous at all. From dusty, dirty rehearsal rooms, to dressing rooms that need more than a lick of paint, the travelling, touring, getting home late at night, the money that you're paid, and the endless physical hard work. It can be day in, day out rejection. You've got to be tough. **Arlene Phillips**

You have to sacrifice a social life. I see at my own school that teenagers get to this age where they discover boys, social life, earrings, handbags, mobile phones and we see a drop-off in attendance. But those aren't the ones that have the instinct to make it all the way to a professional career. **Cassa Pancho**

I was working with a group of third-year students recently. Twenty per cent of them will work, the rest won't, because there just isn't the passion there, there isn't the need. There has to be a need to do this work. **Maxine Doyle**

You have to love it, beyond almost anything, because of the work that goes in, the sacrifices that you have to make, the pain. You get told 'no' a lot. You're putting yourself on the chopping block, you're asking to be criticised, you're told you're not good enough. The love that you have for dancing has to be bigger than all of the negatives. If it's not, then I don't think you should pursue it. **Steven McRae**

If you don't believe that it's your destiny, do something else, because it's too hard otherwise. **Lauren Cuthbertson**

2

The Body

How Important is the 'Perfect Body'?

Dance is a body-fascist art form. There, I've said it. There's no getting around the fact that in dance you are judged on how your body looks as well as what it can do, and both of those things can be as much the result of genetics as they are hard work. Talk to any number of people who didn't quite make their dancing dreams come true and you'll hear the phrase, 'I didn't have the right body.' So what is the perfect body for a dancer? How much does it really matter that you have it? And what can you do if you don't?

The absolutely ideal body, I would say, is a body that has the right proportions. **Arthur Pita**

The idea of having the right body is so that you don't get injured as you delve more and more into the career. If you have the right physique you're going to last longer. **Darcey Bussell**

The body matters a lot. I'm not a skinny-rake ballerina, but it's silly to pretend that not having good proportions and a slender frame doesn't help you. It's just an aesthetic art. **Lauren Cuthbertson**

A lot goes on appearances. It's superficial but people judge so quickly. I was extremely lucky because naturally I had nice feet and I do have natural line. I don't know how. If you're not naturally gifted with the body then you have to have a really solid technique. **Melissa Hamilton**

Having the right body does matter in some aspects. If you want to be a ballerina you need to have feet that have high insteps. You need to be of a certain build so that you can do all the steps without damaging your own body – you can't have fifteen stone of weight driving down into pointe shoes. If you're too heavy, you can't be picked up by a male partner. But if you're doing ballet correctly you will be in shape. **Cassa Pancho**

If you asked every dancer what the perfect body would be, every one would probably give you a different answer. It's like going into an art gallery – you could stare at a painting on the wall and absolutely love it, and the next person will come along and think, 'That does nothing for me.' It's the same with people's bodies. What I think is a beautiful dancer's body, someone else thinks is not. **Steven McRae**

It's different in every place. You go to Russia and everyone has the same look, and it works, but it gives a very similar style of dancing. I like the idea that everyone is different to some extent, but everyone wants long legs and the long neck. **Matthew Golding**

For girls, for classical ballet especially, you have to have an athletic build and strength. **Darcey Bussell**

I always read people saying, 'Oh, I've got a really difficult body,' and then you see them flying around the stage. **Jonathan Goddard**

Shape and size doesn't matter in terms of making dance your life. It does if you want to fit into a corps de ballet and everyone has to look the same, but there are lots of different types of dancing where you don't have to be a skinny size-whatever. Hip hop is great for that. One of the best dancers in our company has got a growth disorder. It doesn't change how good a dancer she is. She's just been accepted into the National Youth Dance Company, on her own merit. **Kate Prince**

The stronger you are in the body, the more animated and articulate you can be in your language of movement. From a hip-hop point of view, it doesn't matter what size you are, if you can do the do, you do the do. If you are agile enough, regardless of size or height, you can do it. **Kenrick Sandy**

When it comes to dance theatre, then you really want to embrace everything. You want to say: 'Wow, she's tiny, but she can really move,' or 'That guy's enormous and I never thought he could be that fast or smooth.' For me as a choreographer, I'm completely attracted to different shapes and sizes and ages. Look at Pina Bausch's company. It's just gorgeous when you see all those different shapes and sizes. **Arthur Pita**

I love differences because I'm always telling stories in my work. I need people who look different to create that world. If everyone looks the same – same height, same body – it doesn't feel like a community. I love having the little guy and the very tall girl. Someone like Michela Meazza, she couldn't get into a ballet company because she was too tall on pointe. But in our company she became a star. **Matthew Bourne**

Every dancer I know has a thing they hate about their body and they work around it, whether it's big thighs or that their feet aren't as arched as they want them to be. I bet even those perfect ballerinas, like Marianela Nuñez, there's probably something she doesn't like. You need to work out what your weaknesses are and work out how to disguise them. There's a lot of smoke and mirrors. **Cassa Pancho**

I was tall for a dancer and it was an issue at first. In the English companies I wasn't seen to fit in. But as society changed and times changed, there were more tall dancers. **Darcey Bussell**

In commercial dance – TV and music videos – image is massively important. It is the prevailing thing. I would say body shape isn't as important any more and you can forge a career with an interesting body, if you use it to your advantage. **Aaron Sillis**

In the commercial dance industry, you will find that if you go up for *X Factor* to be a backing dancer, they'll have a very strict view of what your appearance should be. If you're choosing that environment, you have to make sure you fit. You've got to find the right environment, the right company who will embrace your talent and not your appearance. **Kate Prince**

I look for the kind of body that is right for the show. I was doing the Monty Python *Meaning of Life* reunion and the director wanted very tall girls. For *We Will Rock You* it's very much about characters – physically the bodies can be any shape and type as long as they're strong. For *Saturday Night Fever*, it's about being a diva dancer, about being able to do lifts and be thrown from one boy to another. **Arlene Phillips**

A lot of the best dancers didn't have the best bodies. A lot of these dancers who are told they're not right, they usually do the best because in ballet it's completely about persistence and hard work. A lot of the dancers that had the best bodies don't really last, they just fizzle out. **Matthew Golding**

The body matters, but it doesn't mean that if you don't have it you can't get it. And the sooner you get it – the body's more malleable the younger you are – the more you will achieve. Something like gymnastics really concentrates on that very early on, and you see in dancers that started with gymnastics – in Sylvie Guillem, Alina Cojocaru, Sergei Polunin – that kind of natural ability comes from the fact that they started out doing something that really gave them as much from their body as they could get. **Tamara Rojo**

I think understanding anatomy is a good thing, how things are connected. When you say you've got a tight hamstring, what does that actually mean? If you say you don't have much turnout, what do you actually mean by that? There are solutions. You can work on those tight ligaments. A muscle might be firing too much, not allowing you to open out. Your hip might not be rotating the right way. It's all structure. **Jonathan Goddard**

With dance and sport, it's not necessarily strength or flexibility that's most important. I think, critically, it's balance. I think the key to athletic prowess is some innate, refined, infinitesimal advancement in balance. If you watch Lionel Messi or Roger Federer, they could be literally falling over yet somehow they pull it off. And with dancers, now and again you've got someone who never falls off. **Adam Garcia**

Make the most of what you've got. A dancer has to work on their faults every single day, but they also need to learn how to hide those faults and exploit the assets. You might not have the best turnout, but maybe you have a nice foot, a nice arch. You learn how to create the best line you can with your legs. Other people are born with everything and they're the people that everyone hates. **Steven McRae**

I didn't want to be typecast in the ballets for tall girls, I wanted to be able to do the ballets that were supposed to be only for the petite ones. It was about being able to adapt and look fragile and change the perception of my technique. I would make the step slightly smaller, I wouldn't step out so much, I wouldn't put a hundred per cent into that move because I knew I looked too strong. **Darcey Bussell**

I wasn't built to be a ballet dancer, I'm built to be a sprinter. I've always had brilliant muscle tone, but I've had to work on flexibility and lengthening-out muscles instead of being tight and rigid. I stretch. A lot. My housemate comes home and I'm on the floor stretching in front of the TV. Zone out for half an hour with *Friends* and before you know it, you're done. But do it in a safe way. Be warm. If I'm going to do some stretching at home, I have a hot shower or a hot bath first. **Teneisha Bonner**

I did an audition for the Royal Ballet School at sixteen and got turned down because I was very stiff. That galvanised me a bit. You can definitely do it. Through floor barre technique I explore how I should be working, making adjustments in tiny increments rather than thinking, 'I've got to fit this model of perfection now.' **Jonathan Goddard**

Like in any athletic pursuit, there are the freaks. And I mean that in the nicest possible way. Those who are

genetically blessed more than others. Sylvie Guillem, she's
a freak. Nijinsky was a freak. Nureyev was a freak. Obviously they had great expression as well. That's what makes
them 0.0001% superstars. **Adam Garcia**

Body Conditioning:
Class isn't Enough

Premiership footballers complain of tiredness if they have to play more than a couple of matches a week (and they only train for a few hours a day). Whereas dancers will perform up to eight shows a week, and they train almost every day, all day. Conclusion: dancers are seriously fit. If you want to make it as a pro, just going to your weekly ballet or jazz class won't be enough. You'll need to fine-tune your body. The dancers reveal their secrets for getting into shape.

Definitely try to train outside of just dancing. The only way to do the moves is to condition your body. There are certain training regimes I would do to strengthen my core area, upper body and my legs. A lot of movement I like to do is dynamic and explosive, so my body needs to be able to handle that explosive power. **Kenrick Sandy**

If you want to be a professional dancer you need to be doing your own floor barre, pilates, strength training, fitness training, endurance training, every day. There's no way around it, there's no short cut. Even if one day it's just stretching in front of the telly and then a run around the park, that costs nothing. Nowadays ballet is so competitive, people want super-high legs and fifteen pirouettes on pointe, and you won't get that from a normal ballet class. **Cassa Pancho**

I was always the first person in the building at Rambert, two hours before class. I'd do my own practice, I'd stretch, do a floor barre. I got into qigong recently. I love that time being in the studio on your own, before the other dancers come in and chat, it's special. Then I'm in the zone and ready to go. **Jonathan Goddard**

What's brilliant for stretching is Bikram yoga in forty-degree heat. It's non-impact and I'm building strength and flexibility at the same time, and I feel amazing afterwards. **Teneisha Bonner**

I'm a gym rat, I love the gym. I love to do CrossFit, whatever weights I can find, pilates and gyrotonics, a variety of things to strengthen my body. And when you're injured you shouldn't completely stop, you have to train in different ways. **Matthew Golding**

I've never been into the gym. I'm not someone who enjoys weight training. I cycle a lot, I walk a lot, I run a lot, I climb, do swimming, yoga, pilates. I prefer active sports. **Aaron Sillis**

I always try to use my own body to build up upper-body strength rather than pumping weights. If I can lift myself, I can lift a ballerina. I think a dancer's body can be compared with a lightweight boxer. You want strength and muscle, but you don't want to look bulky. The heavier you are, the more strain it is on your joins and tendons. You want to be lean like a racehorse. **Steven McRae**

As part of my warm-up I do a lot of back raises, sit-ups, press-ups and handstands. I mix that with going climbing or doing martial arts and gymnastics, so I make sure I get my body from all angles. Vary your training. If you keep doing one thing too long your body will stop responding to it. Even when I'm doing the most demanding show, it gets to the point where my body's got used to it, so you need to keep challenging the body. **Tommy Franzén**

If there's a point where you feel tired, just push through it. It's only a bit of pain, nothing's going to break. Get on with it. Almost there! Push! **Teneisha Bonner**

Good Pain:
The Inevitable Gripes

My ballet teacher used to say, 'But it's good pain!' when we were struggling to get our legs into the splits. Does dancing always have to hurt? What's the inside info on skin splits and battered feet? And what about the specific tortures of pointe shoes?

Being a dancer is uncomfortable. I was teaching the other day and I was saying to them, 'For those of you who are interested in doing this professionally, understand: it hurts. And you guys who are doing it for a hobby, that's fine, but it still hurts.' Whichever way you approach it, the common denominator is pain. **Teneisha Bonner**

Everything hurts at some point. But it shouldn't hurt to a level where you are in agony. It is as sore as it must be for people who do the London Marathon or people who work in a physical job. It's not masochistic. Or it should never be a masochistic or sadistic art form. **Tamara Rojo**

I try to get treatments, massage and that sort of thing. If you get a niggle, work on it straight away, rolling on a ball, doing exercises. Get on it quick before it turns into a big problem. If tightness is building up, address it with massage and maybe counteracting exercises to strengthen that part or another part. I learnt anatomy through a sports-massage course. I found it very useful knowing what each muscle does. **Tommy Franzén**

When I feel like my muscles are tired, I do a lot of heat and ice, hot and cold, back and forth to get the blood circulation going. **Matthew Golding**

I like to have a spa day or something, go in the jacuzzi, go to the sauna and the steam room and relax. **Marlon Wallen**

You know what's good pain and you know what's bad pain. Stay away from the bad pain. Stabbing pains – usually not a good sign. Bad pain is when it feels like something is raw, like something is going to break, that's structural; you can't change your structural make-up. The muscular side of things, you can change. If it feels like something's burning, pull back a little bit, breathe into the stretch, get oxygen to the muscles. **Teneisha Bonner**

You do get horrible split skin on your feet sometimes. For those splits I use anti-fungal cream overnight and it takes that stinging redness away. Some people tape up their toes, I just make sure that the skin's hard. Or – this is bad advice – I wear socks and then only take them off for the dress rehearsal. **Jonathan Goddard**

If I'm in trainers I have to make sure that I have orthotic insoles in, to raise my arches. That helps me work through my feet, and get better shock absorption. Make sure your trainers are not too flat. For your knees and your back, impact takes its toll. And I don't do work on my knees unless I have kneepads on. **Teneisha Bonner**

A Word on Pointe Shoes

Don't start pointe work too soon. If you start too soon your legs aren't strong enough for it and you end up going up using your feet, rather than it being your leg muscles that are lifting you. **Lauren Cuthbertson**

Get good shoes that fit you properly. Don't just wear anything off the shelf, ask questions. **Tamara Rojo**

With pointe work, you go through the pain, but there are tips. To prepare for pointe work, if you can bathe your feet in a bucket of water with a couple of capfuls of surgical spirit, it hardens up the skin. And I use a toe pad. When I was younger it was animal wool – you mould it around your foot. **Lauren Cuthbertson**

I remember at school the teachers talking to the girls about not wearing anything in their pointe shoes. Now that my feet are battered old things I'd just say, go through it. **Jonathan Goddard**

I've always learned from what the more experienced dancers do. I remember when I was studying in Spain, Carole Arbo, who was an étoile at the Paris Opera, came as a guest artist and we stole a pair of her pointe shoes – well, she threw them in a bin and we took them and studied them. Now I cut the back of the sole to three quarters, I empty the glue from the sides of the shoes so they're not so stiff. I shellac the front so they are hard where I'm on pointe. **Tamara Rojo**

You have to bang your shoes, to make them less noisy, but that's only for shows. That can make your shoes softer, so if you're training and you're on a budget, you don't want to be banging them to death. **Lauren Cuthbertson**

I remember trying out a thousand ways to tape up my toes so they wouldn't get sore, but in the end I realised the way was just to go through the pain until you become used to it. It's just one of those sacrifices you have to go through for ballet. You've just got to suck it up, that's normally my advice. **Cassa Pancho**

Darning pointe shoes is so time-consuming, but I think the minute you don't care to sew your shoes for the next day, is the minute you don't really care about dancing. I find it quite calming – unless it's five minutes before the *Sleeping Beauty* and you're about to do the Rose Adagio. **Lauren Cuthbertson**

Bad Pain:
When Injury Strikes

From sprains and strains to career-ending trauma, injury can be the plague of a dancer's career. How can you best look after yourself? How do you know when you're pushing yourself too far? Dancers who've been there share what they've learnt about protecting their bodies and coming back from injury.

Injury is an occupational hazard. If you put yourself in the firing line, things may happen. We are pushing our boundaries – creative boundaries, physical boundaries – you can't expect not to get injured. **Teneisha Bonner**

Spend time stretching, not actually dancing but warming up and cooling down. That all plays a part in looking after the body. You can have build-ups of problems in the body that can lead to injuries. **Marlon Wallen**

A really good warm-up is essential. On so many jobs in the commercial world, it's not factored in to the day. When I started working in pop videos we'd start at 10 a.m. and finish at 6 p.m. It's intense all day long, you're thrashing your head around, jumping to your knees, crazy stuff. I'd get in the room beforehand and do a ballet barre. I was eighteen and these seasoned pro dancers came in laughing. They said it had been ages since they'd warmed up. But it shows. Your body will break down more quickly. I'm now thirty-one and I'm still dancing on jobs with nineteen-year-olds and give it just as much as them. I'm like the granddad dancing to Taylor Swift. **Aaron Sillis**

I'm forty-one years old and the reason I still can do what I can do is that I come to class and I finish class. I see people who think they don't need class and then they praise my dancing and I say, 'There's no secret.' The older you get, the more you need to push your body. You do it and you do it and you do it. And then on stage you only have to do it once, it's so easy. **Carlos Acosta**

I think it just comes down to listening to your body, and your body will tell you when you shouldn't push it. Stop if it hurts and do something else. **Matthew Golding**

I think sports massage is really good as injury prevention, if you can afford it. It makes you quite aware of your body. But I wouldn't treat everything a masseur says, or even a physio, as gospel. They're trying to work out what's going on. I think you need to get to know your own body and they can help you get to know it. **Jonathan Goddard**

You need to think about the longevity of your career. Now that I'm over thirty, if I get injured it takes a lot longer to heal than it used to, and nobody's paying my bills. For so many years you are expected to fight and push and fall to the floor and break your body. I'm still willing to work hard, though. Physically I'm stronger than I've ever been, but I'm also more cautious and intelligent about how I work. **Seeta Patel**

I have personal insurance, which not many dancers have, and that helps me to know that I don't really need to wrap myself in cotton wool so much. If something were to happen, I'm covered. I look at my body as a gift, and you have to take care of it, the same way I would look after anything that is close to my heart. My body is my brand. **Teneisha Bonner**

Do a good cool-down after a show so you're not sore the next day. When I get home I love a hot-water bottle. I take painkillers sometimes – I try to stay off them, but they can be really helpful for inflammation. Ice is great if you've banged your knee. Take arnica tablets. And rest. You need to sleep well. **Aaron Sillis**

I've had two serious injuries and one serious illness. It's hell. When it happens you literally don't know if you're going to dance again. This time it was my left foot, an impact injury on stage. I screamed and Carlos [Acosta] carried me off stage. I have nightmares about my injury, sometimes I can almost feel it in my foot. But if I always went on stage thinking this might be the night I suddenly do it again, I wouldn't be able to dance. **Lauren Cuthbertson**

When I had my big injury I was very young in the company. I was doing Romeo, dancing with these incredible ballerinas. Who in their right mind is going to say no to those opportunities? My body was saying no. My Achilles tendon partially ruptured. I was offstage for a year, which was horrendous. I didn't deal with it very well, I was so depressed. I had to work a lot with a sports psychologist to get back on stage. I said, 'I have to get back on stage!' They were like, 'You can't even walk yet.' **Steven McRae**

Don't be a hero. I'm not going on stage if I'm injured, it's not worth it. I think that mentality, dancing through pain – in my line of work that would be called the b-boy mentality – there's one word for it: stupid. I'm not trivialising something that's very close to my heart, but it's only dance. If you don't perform, the only thing that's really going to be bruised a little bit is your pride, your ego. **Teneisha Bonner**

I've had six surgeries. I always looked at injury as a chance to start again. Even after four ankle surgeries I was excited to start again. And while I'm sitting there and I can't move my legs, I'll work on my upper body. You can do something else. **Matthew Golding**

Use your time wisely. I spent the first six months of my year off injured feeling sorry for myself, and then I went to the other extreme and became so proactive, decided I wanted to start studying, I was going to take on the world. I'd say to someone in the same position, 'It's unfortunate, but it's happened. How are you going to deal with it?' **Steven McRae**

I had a bit of a nightmare a few years ago with my first serious injury which was slightly misdiagnosed. It's hard to trust even a specialist, because they can't feel your body. I shopped around for another surgeon and I learnt all the terminology. You have to be able to have a dialogue that you feel comfortable with and you have to question everything – and don't feel fazed because he's the doctor. **Lauren Cuthbertson**

Sprained ankles, pulled hamstrings, back problems, neck problems, shoulder problems. I see it all as an opportunity for learning and I try to explore movement that I can do with that injury, modifying moves, coming up with new moves without using that arm or that leg. Take the opportunity to explore a new way of moving. **Tommy Franzén**

If you can just stay sane and forgive the universe and all of that, then it's okay. And then you have to work like a dog. It's graft like nothing else. It's agony and you don't recognise yourself. You're suddenly terrible at something you're meant to be good at. But the body is like putty. If you're good to it you can achieve so much. And if you push it and beg it to do what you want it to do, it can. It's a living thing. In a very simple way, anything can heal. **Lauren Cuthbertson**

Injury could happen tomorrow, or tonight. Who knows? So I think the most important thing is to enjoy dancing while it's happening. For so long I was focused on what was coming next, and we work too bloody hard not to grasp the moments that we have. **Melissa Hamilton**

I found a nice mentality when I was coming back from being sick. I didn't see progress day to day, didn't even see progress week to week, but monthly it was always just getting a little bit better. It's all in the right direction. I think the body and mind have an amazing way of dealing with things. Like when people have babies and then forget the pain. Injury and illness is like that. Once you're free again and on that stage, it's: 'Here I am!' **Lauren Cuthbertson**

You Are What You Eat

It's a myth that dancers don't eat. A dancer who wants to have a long, healthy career can't survive on coffee and cigarettes. Nutrition is a keyword in dance training these days, so what fuel do our dancers put in their temple-like bodies? Gummy bears get the thumbs-up, and maybe it's time to buy a bullet blender...

Being a dancer you want to maintain as great health as possible. I'm not advocating being really skinny, you just need to be really healthy. Make sure you're getting enough of the right proteins. Dance is such an intensive activity you need to be refuelling your body with the right things, lots of water, cutting out the sugary drinks. We love coffee, but don't over-caffeinate yourself or you'll get dehydrated. **Aaron Sillis**

Your diet is extremely important. My wife [dancer Elizabeth Harrod] and I love food, and we love a nice drink, but it's everything in moderation. Obviously if I go home and have a whole cake and a packet of crisps every night then I'm probably not going to look so hot in a white unitard. If you're on your feet exercising for almost twelve hours a day, you can basically eat what you want – but if you pump yourself full of junk you're not going to last long. **Steven McRae**

Over the years I used to eat a lot of rubbish and never put weight on. But when you start getting into your thirties you start putting on that weight and it's hard to get rid of, so it's important to have a healthy diet and eat well. Most people say more protein, less carbs. Right now I'm eating chicken and fish and I don't eat a lot of red meat. You can have your healthy carbs: sweet potato, brown bread, brown rice. And I eat a lot of fruit and veg, a lot of salad. **Kenrick Sandy**

When I do my food shopping I buy good carbs like quinoa, millet, amaranth, rye bread, brown rice. I try to limit the wheat and gluten and also lactose. I order a box of organic vegetables. I make sure that the food I've got at home is really healthy, but then when I go out I have the naughty stuff as well – I love cake and chocolate – but I make my habits healthy and surround myself with the good stuff. **Tommy Franzén**

Don't mess around with your diet when you're a teenager. It'll mess you up. I saw it happen when I was young. It becomes this obsession and the biggest gossip of the dance class is what people have got in their lunchbox. You need the energy to work hard and if you mess up your metabolism when you're younger you've got less chance of being able to maintain that when you're older. You're growing and you need the strength and your bones need the nourishment. **Lauren Cuthbertson**

Young dancers shouldn't play the game of dieting. If you start playing around with diet at a young age, if you starve yourself, it can really affect you in the long term. You can play the game now, but you won't last. **Matthew Golding**

I eat all the time. I try to snack on good stuff – nuts, fruit – but, that said, if I feel like some sweets, I have them. I won't deprive myself. **Teneisha Bonner**

You just want to eat the right kind of calories. For me it's important to get enough protein so I can repair my body. Protein builds muscle. What really helps if you want to drop your weight a bit is to limit carbs – I don't believe in cutting things out completely, but limit it, especially in the evenings. Have more protein and salad and lots of vegetables in the evening and good carbs in the day. **Tommy Franzén**

Have a treat day. It shakes your body up. A treat day's actually healthy. Anything that you do regularly, your body gets immune to. You need to shock your body by doing something different. It's like a reset button. **Marlon Wallen**

At the Royal Ballet School you had breakfast, you had lunch, you had dinner. At four o'clock you had tea and two biscuits. After homework you had your tuck box – either chocolate or some sweets with a hot chocolate or a cup of tea. That's a structure and it just worked. We all did that. **Lauren Cuthbertson**

I bought a bullet blender. It's the best money I've ever spent. I blend everything those blades can chop: kale, banana, kiwis, almonds, cashews, an egg, and then take it to work with me. It metabolises into your system so much more quickly. If I start the day off well, then chances are I'm good. **Teneisha Bonner**

On a show day I'm fairly specific about eating. It's difficult because you'd normally have class around 12. Then I would try to eat something small, a banana, and then we'd do rehearsals till 5.30/6. Sometimes there are breaks, fifteen minutes, and I'd eat a sandwich or something. Show days are tough because there's not a proper break. **Jonathan Goddard**

I need at least an hour and a half before a show. You get that break after company class to have dinner and I like to eat immediately so I have time to digest. Before the show, I used to have this ritual of eating two shortbread fingers, for a little bit of sugar. And then in the interval it's always a banana, maybe an energy drink. Sugar's good in the interval – gummy bears or cola bottles, just a handful to give you a sugar fix. Then post-show it's usually protein. Some fish, some veg, lean and light, but I need to give myself something back. **Aaron Sillis**

With the high-intensity stuff you just have to keep going. I think athletes often have a coffee for a kick, a quick boost. While I'm performing I'd normally have a banana and a Coke or a Lucozade – I'm not going to recommend that to young people, they can have the banana. **Jonathan Goddard**

Some people don't like to eat before a show. I know loads of girls who will just eat broccoli before a show, which is ridiculous. I love to eat before a show. I really enjoy sushi – it's light, it's clean, it doesn't weigh you down too much. I've had times when all the boys go for pizza and pasta and garlic bread and then you've got no energy for the show. Those thick, starchy, carb-heavy foods don't work for me. **Aaron Sillis**

It's important to vary your diet. Too much of anything is not good, even broccoli. **Tommy Franzén**

3
Getting a Job

Adam Garcia

Having the Right Attitude

Having a strong technique is one thing, but the strength you need to build a career in dance is as much mental as it is physical. Persistence and resilience are key attributes for a dancer, whether that's for dealing with knock-backs, or pushing your career to the next level. Our dancers say, it's all in the attitude…

From a young age, if I was told I couldn't do something I'd think, 'I'm going to prove you wrong.' Then everything would be one hundred per cent effort till I proved them wrong. I think that has been my driving force in my career. **Aaron Sillis**

I only got some of the things Ballet Black has by being very persistent. Or pushy, depending which way you look at it. **Cassa Pancho**

I was very lucky to be in two West End shows while I was in college. I remember people saying, 'Oh, you get every job you go for.' I didn't. I just went for a lot of jobs. **Stephen Mear**

It's about just doing it. Doing something until you fall. I had a teacher who always said, 'You're not working hard enough if you don't fall.' **Darcey Bussell**

The dancers in Ballet Black are competitive with each other, but it's quite an open sort of competition. There's no glass in the pointe shoes, nothing like that. There's no sabotage. **Cassa Pancho**

My ballet teacher was an amazing woman, but she told me that all I was ever going to end up doing was dancing on a podium in Soho in a pair of gold hotpants. When I was in *Men in Motion* with Ivan Putrov I was dancing with stars of the Bolshoi, the Mariinsky. I texted her and said, 'Just thought you'd like to know I'm closing Ivan Putrov's show in Moscow tonight.' I've since heard that that text made her year. **Aaron Sillis**

In *Can We Talk About This?*, one of the dancers got injured and my workload tripled overnight. It wasn't created on me, but I was able to meet the challenge. I'd like to think that if you spoke to Lloyd Newson [Artistic Director of DV8] he'd say he saw my ability to push and fight for those things that I wan't necessarily trained in or natural in. I attribute that to the fire I've had to have working as a freelancer. There is that constant trying to dig deep. **Seeta Patel**

There's a big difference between ambitious and obnoxious. There's nothing wrong with being ambitious, not in the sense of wanting to stab somebody in the back, but in the sense of wanting to be good. The English lack that. I've worked in America and they're really ambitious. I strive to be one of the best choreographers and I don't hesitate saying that. I know that shocks a few people. I'm not saying I'm the best. I'm just saying I want to keep up with everybody. **Stephen Mear**

I'm one of those people where nothing is ever good enough. I came into ballet late so I was playing catch-up and trying to learn everything as fast as possible, go, go, go! That served me well and made it possible to progress, but I'm never happy with the level I'm at. What changed recently is that I have to learn to be content with what it is in the moment. But still next time I want it to be better. **Melissa Hamilton**

Making mistakes, that's part of the job. It's all about taking risks. Don't be safe. A lot of dancers would say, 'Oh, I can't do that.' There is a lot of fear factor. I was happy to make mistakes. I was happy to throw myself into something and make a fool of myself. It wasn't about always doing everything perfectly straight away. You have to test yourself and see. **Darcey Bussell**

Don't be afraid of failing. A lot of people won't do things like auditions because they're afraid of being told no. But most dancers have been told 'no' more than they have 'yes'. Countless times. It's a case of taking it and brushing it off and then carrying on. Just go for it, get stuck in straight away. Don't be embarrassed. Don't hide or shy away from any opportunities that present themselves. **Matthew Rees**

When somebody says, 'No, no, we can't do that, it's impossible,' I feel my hackles go up. I say, 'Let's just try it.' **Stephen Mear**

When we think we're doing something perfectly it becomes safe-looking. You have to think, how far can I push this step, how far can I go off-balance, can I squeeze in another turn? You should always be attempting the next stage and not be satisfied with the first stage. It is a frame of mind. **Darcey Bussell**

Be prepared to fail. Even now sometimes I struggle, but it's just going for it anyway, knowing that you're going to fall over sometimes. Nobody's going to laugh at you. **Matthew Rees**

I don't know about this 'fake it till you make it' thing. If you don't know, go and ask someone. I think the dance world is very generous and if you ask for help, someone will help you. **Cassa Pancho**

Be fearless and open. I've seen dancers that aesthetically perhaps don't look the best, their technique is not the strongest, but they go on stage and you don't doubt them. You know they're going to do it, they're going to give a performance. It might not be flawless, but they do it, they do it well. A lot of people get a long way by having that approach. Choreographers and directors are naturally attracted to people who throw themselves in head-first. **Steven McRae**

Being Employable

Time after time, the choreographers and directors I spoke to for this book emphasised that the people they hire aren't just good dancers, they're good people. They're the faces you want to turn up and see every day – dancing is a job, after all, and these are your colleagues. So what matters most to employers and how can you make sure you're the dancer everyone wants to work with?

Have respect for everybody in the industry because you never know when you're going to come across them. Never have attitude – this business is too small. It's amazing how things get around. I get called up by many directors asking what people are like. **Stephen Mear**

You have to treat everybody equally. Some people speak down to a dresser, or anyone who isn't the choreographer or director, they disregard them as not being a worthwhile connection. But everyone knows everyone, the backstage technicians, stage management, stage door. Those people have probably been doing it a lot longer than you, know a lot more people than you, and so you have to have a good reputation. **Aaron Sillis**

I was twenty-one when the company started and I wanted everyone to be 'nice', and then I realised that's not always possible. It is important to me that a dancer in my company is a good human being, and that can mean that everyone is cordial in the studio and then we go home and have our own separate lives. **Cassa Pancho**

I always say I like divas on stage but not off. You want people to come out and take the stage, but behind the scenes you want them to say thank you to the dressers. **Matthew Bourne**

I think being on stage you are exposed one hundred per cent. Nice people come across on stage in a different way to people who are closed or who have angst and personal issues. Being able to reach out into your audience, the more open you are the better. And the more comfortable you are with yourself, the more open you are. **Melissa Hamilton**

The people I want to work with again and again are people who always show up on time and they don't have lots of dramas that they bring to work. I just want you to be in the room, be positive, be on board. The people you want to work with are the people who cause you the least trouble. I'm not your babysitter, I'm not your mum. This is a job. **Kate Prince**

Be on time. (I'm late, always.) **Matthew Golding**

If you want to make your way up, you don't ask questions, you just do. Unless you're a naturally god-given talent like Baryshnikov, you keep your head down and work. You do as you're told, especially at the beginning of your career. Find your feet and only then can you start trying to make waves. Unless you're Sylvie Guillem. Then you can do whatever you want. **Melissa Hamilton**

Don't get cocky, don't get arrogant. You're not better than anyone else. Just do the work. I've discovered working in film and theatre that you've got to be a team player so everyone likes to work with you. **Adam Garcia**

Don't ever think you're better than someone just because you've got the main part. You've just had that lucky break. It's fortune. **Darcey Bussell**

I look for someone who's got a great work ethic, who's going to get on with the job and get on with people. People get confused and think, 'I'm the best dancer in the world, I'm going to push forward with that.' But it's not enough. You need to be a good person to work with, friendly, a team player. Managing yourself well is just as important as learning the dance side of it. **Aaron Sillis**

I tend to surround myself with positive people, people that can inspire me, people I can look at and think: this is the reason I'm doing what I'm doing. Is it good to have some healthy competition? Absolutely, one hundred per cent. **Marlon Wallen**

Be professional. Be respectful. Don't feel you're above the job. Sometimes on a production things might not happen the way you thought they would, things may go wrong, and as a performer you might think, 'Well, it's got nothing to do with me.' But the more you show support for what you're involved in, the nicer an experience it becomes. **Kenrick Sandy**

Everyone has a moany day, a bad day. But just knock yourself out of it. I said to one company that were moaning about rehearsals, 'You know what? You'll have plenty of time to moan when you're out of work.' That shut them up in two seconds. **Stephen Mear**

Networking and Getting Noticed

Nobody is going to give you a job if they don't know you're out there. How can a dancer in the corps de ballet stand out when their job is to fit in? How does a freelancer get themselves noticed? Do you have to have an agent? And is there an alternative to the dreaded 'networking'? The dancers can give you some tips...

One way of getting noticed is to have a kick-ass technique. If you go to a class and you can do more pirouettes than everybody else, and your legs are higher than everybody else, and you can jump higher than everybody else, people will notice. The truth is, if you are a good dancer, people will notice. That's the good thing about ballet, it is meritocratic. **Tamara Rojo**

If a choreographer or director came in when we were doing a class, I made sure that I would always do everything four times instead of two. It's about showing your keenness and your desire to improve, improve, improve. They want to know that you're hungry and you're listening to every word from the teacher. They want to see you responding and changing as you're given corrections. You have to show that you are motivated to learn. **Darcey Bussell**

At fourteen I ended up doing a musical. My sister was in it and someone dropped out. They'd seen me dance at the opening-night party. Even though I didn't know it at the time, I think I attracted it, if you know what I mean. It happened for a reason. You do create your own luck. I don't think it was just by accident. **Tommy Franzén**

When you're in the corps de ballet, you can still stand out in class. If someone goes off ill and you have to go on in their place, you don't wait for someone to say, 'Okay, your rehearsal is at this time.' You already have the music on your iPod at night, you know your part inside out. **Lauren Cuthbertson**

Pushiness is an interesting subject. I work with so many people now – this year we had three companies going at the same time, a hundred dancers – and the people who keep on my radar are more likely to be in my head when I'm casting something. It's clever to remind people you're there. Go and see their show and say hello, or write them a nice message. It's very good for choreographers to hear you love their work. It sounds narcissistic but it's not. It's just great to work with people who are as excited as you are. **Matthew Bourne**

A few of the lads from school made a piece and we entered it to Youth Dance England. We got to perform it and Michael Nunn and Billy Trevitt from BalletBoyz were there. So we plucked up some courage and went over to them and said, 'We're seriously impressed with what you guys do and we'd love to work with you.' And they asked us to go into the studio with them. If we didn't ask that day, I wouldn't be here now. I think a bit of front and a bit of luck is the ultimate combination. **Matthew Rees**

A lot of the time you do need an agent for commercial work. Contemporary dancers generally don't have agents but musical theatre, yes. I've probably been on the books of over twenty agents. Each agent gets certain jobs. The producer might decide he's going to go with three agents, so if you're only on the books of one that's not chosen, you miss out. **Tommy Franzén**

There are lots of commercial agents and you can have multiple agents. Get on all the agencies, get on Spotlight, join Equity. **Aaron Sillis**

Get yourself out there. Go to classes where you know there are choreographers or people who are doing shows. Get yourself to auditions, get yourself into agencies, get pictures done, get a CV done. Constantly have your ear to the ground to hear what's going on. Use social media. Look at what events are coming up and get your name considered before anyone else. **Kenrick Sandy**

Go to classes at Pineapple, at The Place. Learn who's choreographing, see who's out there making work. Go and see lots of theatre, learn who the directors are. **Aaron Sillis**

Networking is good, but that cuts out a whole swathe of people who are much more introverted. I think you should approach networking in a global sense. Going to workshops is a brilliant way to get jobs. Take interest in a company and go to class with them. Find out a little bit about the dancers, whether you know anyone who knows one of those dancers. It's all through networks, but I don't mean going up to someone and saying, 'I love your work, can I come and work for you?' **Jonathan Goddard**

I don't know how to schmooze. I'm really bad at that. If you put me in a room with people, I will stand in the corner by myself and wait for the night to be over. **Cassa Pancho**

Networking's such a horrible world. We got told that a lot at college: you need to network, you need to meet people. I never approached it that way. I think if you do it right, networking happens very naturally. You meet people on jobs, you have an interest in what they do, you make a connection. It has to feel genuine – that's when people will hire you. **Aaron Sillis**

Send a polite email with a very specific focus. Find out a bit about the company. If you know they take class, ask if you can take class with them. The more general the request, the harder it is to reply to. The more specific the better: 'Is it possible to meet you next Tuesday for a cup of tea?' *That* I can reply to. Or: 'I'm coming to see your show, can I meet you afterwards for five minutes?' A really specific request that's feasible and doesn't take too much effort. **Jonathan Goddard**

Now it is easier to keep connections going with social media. Even before you've left a job you've got friend requests. You can follow people's careers and keep up to date with what they're up to. Classes get filmed and posted online, and if you go to the class and you get chosen to perform at the end, you're going to be seen by thousands of people. **Aaron Sillis**

Apply a business mentality to what you love doing. Any dance events going on, anything that could enhance your career, anywhere for you to be seen, you need to be going there and taking part and getting involved. You need to be on LinkedIn, Facebook, Twitter, so that people are engaged with what you're doing day to day. We've had companies contact us for work through Twitter. **Marlon Wallen**

Definitely have a showreel. Most of us have our own YouTube channel. Social media is useful, but I don't think it's necessary. These days I do tweet, but I'm not very active any more. I found I spent a lot of time being on social media and it wasn't leading me in any direction. So I decided to put that to one side. If you want to get work, it's more valuable to be in a class. **Tommy Franzén**

Nailing Auditions

Your stomach lurching as you wait for your name to be called out; the elation of getting the part; the cruel blow of getting cut – auditions might be the most nail-biting part of a dancer's life, and sometimes the most disheartening. Everybody has to audition at some point, and even the most successful dancers have stories of failure, but we have plenty of insider's advice on how to make the best of every audition, and increase your chances of success.

1. How to Prepare; What to Wear

First, you've got to try to get an audition. What do you write when you write in to a company? Well the big no-nos are standard letters. 'Dear Sir/Madam' almost always goes straight in the bin. 'I saw your production and it made me feel that I'd love to work with you' – they go in the 'yes' pile straight away. You've got so much choice, all the little things become important. **Matthew Bourne**

You should only send in a photograph of yourself looking like yourself. Sometimes dancers send photographs of themselves in the splits, or smoking a cigarette in hot-pants, and it's really off-putting. It doesn't have to be an expensive photograph, just a realistic headshot of you looking like you. **Maxine Doyle**

We've got a collection in the office of the weirdest photos we've been sent over the years, of people doing the oddest things. You want to have some dance shots and also have a nice portrait. Look natural, look inviting as a person. **Matthew Bourne**

You need to do your research on the audition. Know the choreographer's work or the production so you've got some knowledge of what they like. Dress appropriately – maybe you need to ask your agent, get the right brief. Ask friends what they're wearing and take multiple options. Have every dance shoe in your bag. Take a towel. **Aaron Sillis**

In America, one thing I noticed is that they make it their business to know what they are auditioning for and who the creative team are. I thought it was a joke that they knew who I was. Do your homework. **Stephen Mear**

Americans can teach us a lot about auditions. They come in looking fantastic, as if it's a performance. If you're going for a particular role, make yourself look right for that show. When we were auditioning for Mary Poppins, some quite famous women came in looking a bit like Mary Poppins – the hair up, a blouse on, a bit prim – leading you to think you could see them in that role. They knew what they were doing. **Matthew Bourne**

You have to be the one people look at in an audition. You have a roomful of however many girls and you have to instantly make your mark, be that from the leotard you wear, how you do your hair... something that people want to look at. You can't be like everybody else. **Melissa Hamilton**

Definitely try to stand out in some way, without being over the top. Make an impact from the get-go. **Tommy Franzén**

I think what you wear is really subjective. Sometimes people wear bizarre outfits – big flowery trousers or really sexy things – and often that doesn't help. I just like being able to see people looking quite simple, so I can get a sense of them as people. That said, someone recently came in in a sort of négligée and tracksuit bottoms, and she was amazing, she could carry it off. But some choreographers have a very particular aesthetic. If you're going to do an audition in Belgium it's probably useful to have lots of facial hair! **Maxine Doyle**

You need to make your legs look fabulous. **Stephen Mear**

Be prepared to strip down if you need to. How much you take off? It depends how European the audition is! If you're a guy you probably want to wear some running shorts, so they can see your legs. Or tights. I've seen it so many times that people are unzipped at the most pressurised moment and they don't have anything on underneath. **Jonathan Goddard**

Be confident in who you are and understand that you're nobody else. That may sound very simple, but I've been to quite a few auditions and you see the trends – loads of blondes, loads of redheads, loads of black girls with the same weave. If you want to stick out and make an impression, don't go with that trend. Understand what works for you and your body and what makes you shine. **Teneisha Bonner**

I make sure I'm really warmed up and focused. I think about it all morning, listen to good music. Put yourself in a good place, it's so much about that. Listen to good tunes that are uplifting – I really like funk tracks – that gets me really happy. If I'm happy I definitely do a better audition. **Tommy Franzén**

Always turn up with your CV up to date. Make sure you've got the right contact details on it. I can't tell you the amount of people we've lost, or we've had to track down, because of an email or phone-number error. They're silly things, but they're really important. **Maxine Doyle**

Build up some experience in auditioning. That's a technique in itself. See it as a fun thing. You have to do a lot of them, so you may as well have fun and think you're there to learn something. Then you're going to go out of that audition feeling wiser, whether you get the job or not. **Tommy Franzén**

2. Making a Good Impression

I look at a dancer from the moment they enter the room. As they walk in, what is the first thing they do? Do they stand around gossiping? I always watch how people learn, how they pick up the choreography, how they take instruction. **Arlene Phillips**

With auditions, you really just have to think: how can I stand out? What can make me look different to everyone else? Is it what I wear, is it my attitude? Is it the research I've done? Treat an audition how you would an interview. Your first impression is what they're looking at. You really need to be bold and look like you know what you're doing, even if you're not one hundred per cent sure. You need to be able to sell it. **Marlon Wallen**

Turn your phone off. That's a real bugbear. **Aaron Sillis**

The first and foremost thing is etiquette. I hate it when you're standing ready to do the audition and someone stands in front of you. How rude. Sometimes people come with such a horseracing mentality: there's the finish line. I get it, you want to get that job. But bring that person over to you by bringing a positive attitude to what you're doing. The commercial scene is a very dog-eat-dog world and people are out for themselves. **Kenrick Sandy**

It's definitely difficult at the beginning of a routine to be strong. They're going to judge you so quickly. Try to get in the front row, don't hide behind other people, but obviously be respectful. Elbows – it does happen, but I don't believe in that, I rely on my own talent. I never want it to be that I got a job because I elbowed myself to the front. I want it to be because I did a really good job at the audition. **Tommy Franzén**

Do not stand at the back bitching about the people who've got themselves to the front. Because you will always be that person at the back bitching. You have to push yourself, wear blinkers, do your best. Even if you don't get the job, if you can come out saying you really did your best, there's nothing more refreshing. People will remember you for other jobs. **Stephen Mear**

A sense of wanting to be there and being enthusiastic about doing the work together is very important. **Hofesh Shechter**

Channel nerves in the right way. For me it's about not getting too distracted. When you're in a room for an audition with fifty to a hundred dancers, if you're too focused on what everyone else is doing, your nerves will override. You need to keep in the zone. It's almost like meditation. Listen to the choreographer, get your energy calm and together and channel it into the dance. You need to get your head out of the idea that there are people watching and just perform. **Aaron Sillis**

Move around a lot, don't just stay in one place. Being at the back is not great. I would normally stand at the front to one side, but that can be a blind spot, so keep moving around, but don't elbow people out of the way. **Jonathan Goddard**

Some people come and they hide in the corner like they don't want to be seen and you think, 'Well, I don't want to see you either.' **Matthew Bourne**

I'd recommend not sitting down. Maybe if you've got a long audition it's more acceptable, but if it's quite a quick audition process and someone's sat at the side it does give the impression they're a bit bored. Body language is important. Don't fold your arms and close yourself off. **Aaron Sillis**

I've been on both sides of auditions and exams, and when somebody's very stressed, but they force it out-wards as an armour it can be quite repellent. You want to be open and receptive, smiling and listening. Not just *looking* like you're listening – but actually listening *and* thinking. **Jonathan Goddard**

What impresses me are people who are attentive to what they're doing, who will listen to the ballet master or mis-tress, will attempt corrections, ask intelligent questions, won't go in a huff because they haven't got it. Finding the solution, not the problem, is great. And people in the interview who clearly have read about the company. Not people who sit down and say, 'So, what do you do?' I'm not the one who's here to be interviewed. **Cassa Pancho**

Some people talk a lot in auditions, which is very frustrating. Keep quiet, be conscientious, ask questions that are relevant – but don't ask too many questions. That's really annoying when someone asks silly questions that have been answered already. **Aaron Sillis**

One thing that puts me off straight away is if someone is disrespectful or bullying with other members of the group they're in, even if that person is clearly not very good. I don't need an eye roll if they think that person isn't any good and it's affecting them. I need that person to solve the problem. **Wayne McGregor**

I watch people when they're not dancing as much as when they are. Sometimes we'll put them in pairs and see how they are with each other. I famously gave one boy a job who thought he'd done the worst audition ever. He had a really terrible partner, but he was so gentlemanly and nice and polite with her, even though he could feel his own audition going to pot. All those things become important when you know you've got to spend time together, touring around the country, around the world. **Matthew Bourne**

I can tell you what not to do in a company audition. Do not come in chewing gum. Do not come up to the desk and say, 'I didn't bring my pointe shoes.' Don't complain about anything. Don't sit there for twenty minutes talking about the company you wanted to join, but you didn't get in and that's why you're at the Ballet Black audition. And don't trash other companies or directors because, even if I agree, I know that you will then go and trash me and my company at your next audition. That's a really big no-no. **Cassa Pancho**

3. Delivering a Knockout Performance

Jump the highest, perform hard. It does work if you go slightly beyond what you would feel comfortable with, just to get noticed. **Tommy Franzén**

I've said to people in auditions, even if you think this is the worst piece of choreography, make me think it's the best thing you've ever done. You can get away with so much if you go with your full heart and passion. **Stephen Mear**

It isn't always about being the very best dancer, but it's about grabbing people's attention – the choreographer, the creators, the director, the dance masters. It's about grabbing their attention and it's about focus, a tremendous amount of focus. **Arlene Phillips**

Sometimes it's not necessarily about doing anything bigger than the other person. Sometimes it is about your character, your flavour. When you're smiling and you seem warm, people are drawn to you straight away. Because as a dancer you're not talking, they need to be able to pick up that energy. **Marlon Wallen**

The mirror can be quite distracting, when you start focusing too much on what you look like. I like to look through the mirror, or beyond the mirror, and imagine that there's no one else in the room and just perform. **Aaron Sillis**

People come into an audition and yes they can do the steps, yes the feet are moving, yes the arms are moving, but what is the body saying? The people that strike you, their eyes are bright, they're alert and they're focusing, not just on getting the movement of the feet or arms right, but on exactly what the body is expressing. **Arlene Phillips**

I've always found that if I go to an audition and just enjoy it, more often than not, they will enjoy me enjoying it, even if I get something wrong. Performance covers a multitude of sins. You could be technically brilliant, but if you're not connecting – it's usually the eyes – it's null and void. **Teneisha Bonner**

There's nothing you can do actively, I don't think, to stand out. I remember when I did auditions, I thought if it was right, if there was a connection, then it would happen. I don't want to force it, get the job and then live with that forced connection. People think, 'I'm going to go to this audition and my life might change.' But I don't believe life is going to change because of one event and I think people who think that are a bit melodramatic about the whole experience. **Hofesh Shechter**

One piece of advice: be yourself. Don't put on a persona of what you think a dancer should be like. There are lots of people who are po-faced, that's so off-putting. Be natural. If you do something wrong, laugh about it. You want to work with real people who you're going to have a good time with. **Matthew Bourne**

People always say 'be yourself', but that's really difficult because the point is you're trying to be what they want. **Jonathan Goddard**

4. What They're Looking For

This might sound strange, but what I'm looking for is a normal person, who would have a conversation with you, look you in the eye and be genuinely curious and open. Someone who would have interests outside of dance and not be too myopic. I'm interested in a body that is clearly very well trained, where there's a clear mastery over the body, but the humanistic thing is very important. It bewilders me how any people come into an audition and don't look at you. **Wayne McGregor**

I recently led auditions for some students, and the people that stood out, yes they were great dancers, but when I talked to them in the break, they were also the dancers where you could see their life experience in their dancing – even if they were only twenty-one or twenty-two – and they weren't afraid of offering that and sharing it. **Maxine Doyle**

It doesn't matter to me where they stand or what they're wearing. That kind of superficial stuff doesn't interest me. **Wayne McGregor**

In four seasons of *Got to Dance*, out of 1,500 auditions, I can remember maybe forty. They're the ones that made you feel something. It's when you relinquish yourself. When someone can really let go and be free in terms of just dancing, just really being in that moment. That's endlessly watchable. Not when people go, 'I'm emoting!' and they're very good at looking like they're smelling some farts. But when they're *in* it. **Adam Garcia**

I'm never impressed by someone who stands at the barre and kicks their leg up fifty thousand times. I'm interested in the one who might say a quiet hello and be very intelligently engaged in the whole audition process. I don't think the audition is a place to show off all the things that you can do in the first five minutes. You see that a lot in improvisation, they want to show what their schtick is. What's important is that you offer something of yourself and want to get something out of that experience. **Wayne McGregor**

Often the most talented people are a little quirky, a little bit eccentric. We've lost that a bit in the dance world. In the seventies and eighties in the Royal Ballet, the dancers were characters and personalities. Let your *self* come into your dancing. Express yourself through movement, don't just follow the pack and be the same. **Matthew Bourne**

I must have seen thousands of young dancers in the UK and the US. We look for people who are good dancers – within our style – are dynamic, have a good use of the floor, energy, a sense of risk. But beyond that, I'm most interested in presence and charisma and confidence. And I'm interested in dancers who are interested in telling stories and expressing something physically, and who aren't frightened of acting. **Maxine Doyle**

You cannot not be a triple threat now in musical theatre. You only get one chance when there are so many people auditioning. **Stephen Mear**

Charisma. Some people have 'it', they have a charm and energy. But it's interesting, we have a show that's been running for four years in New York and we're in a process of recasting every six months. I've seen dancers come back three or four times, and by the fifth time they've been ready and they've been right. There are definitely certain things that can change. **Maxine Doyle**

5. Dealing with Rejection

Probably the biggest mistake is to take it to heart too much. A lot of people finish their dancing career after their first, second, third audition. They're heartbroken, their confidence just goes. But you have to do a minimum of ten to have even tried, maybe twenty. If you've just come out of dance college at nineteen and you don't get booked for jobs, sometimes it might be because you look too young. But if you've got the talent, after a few years, you'll make the break. **Tommy Franzén**

If you've given it your all and you don't get the job, you just have to say: I wasn't right for this job, but I am determined that I will continue. I will not see this as a huge backward step, but another process of learning. If you're constantly looking back, you're constantly destroying yourself. You have to be forward-thinking. **Arlene Phillips**

As a dancer, or an actor, you are going to hear 'no' a lot more than you hear 'yes'. It's not always personal. Sometimes they might have a point, maybe you do need to work on this a bit more, maybe that's what's holding you back. But be prepared to hear 'no' ninety per cent of the time. I audition still for things and I don't get them. Realistically, if I get three jobs out of, let's say, fifty auditions a year, I'm a six per cent strike rate. But I get work. **Adam Garcia**

It's persistence. You have to grow a thick skin, rhino skin, because the amount of rejection you can have – even if you're successful – it's a huge amount. Probably getting one out of ten auditions that you go for is normal. **Tommy Franzén**

It can be really upsetting being cut in an audition, but as a reassurance, I've done many auditions and not got a lot of them. I've never gone to an open audition and got anywhere. **Jonathan Goddard**

There's always another job. **Adam Garcia**

Competitions:
A Good Idea?

From the Prix de Lausanne to Britain's Got Talent, *there's no denying that winning a major dance competition is one way to launch your career. Or is it the taking part that counts? The dancers who've won, and lost, share their thoughts.*

The best way to get performance experience is to do competitions. I was on stage almost every weekend at the age of eight or nine. It teaches you a lot, being exposed at such a young age: what it feels like to win, and also what it's like to lose – you learn very quickly that you can't win everything. You learn what it's like to be on stage and forget the routine (keep going, improvise), about costume malfunctions (keep going), when the music stops (keep going). **Steven McRae**

Competitions are terrifying and it's awful. And competing in an artistic world is messed up, because it's just opinions. But I never did competitions to win. I knew the experience I gained would benefit me way more than sitting on my ass during the holidays. **Melissa Hamilton**

In the hip-hop world, there are loads of dance battles and some dancers are known worldwide from doing those battles. It's definitely a way of getting known. **Tommy Franzén**

I did freestyle disco dancing and I thought it was great to compete. You had to be creative. The judges walk around and you're on the dance floor with two hundred other kids. It's insane. You had to strike a pose on the dance floor – how do you play that game? I remember walking on very slowly to have more command, playing little tricks like that. I think that made me think about how to be on stage. **Arthur Pita**

I think doing TV talent shows like *Britain's Got Talent* is a great experience, from my perspective. Flawless started from nowhere and we've worked with a lot of big names. We're still humbled by the experiences we've been able to have. It's crazy. **Marlon Wallen**

Doing *So You Think You Can Dance?* really was a good experience. I don't think doing a TV talent show would do any harm, most of the time, although they do like to make a story out of you – I was worried it was going to ruin my reputation. But these days I would say that reality TV programmes are not as effective because they've been around for so long that no one's a star any more. **Tommy Franzén**

Darcey Bussell

4

In the Studio

What Choreographers Want

Creating work in the studio with a choreographer can be one of the most rewarding parts of a dancer's career, but every choreographer's process is different. On some jobs, dancers have a huge amount of input, developing movement material through tasks and collaboration. On others, their role is to perform the steps exactly as the choreographer has set them. What happens when you get in the studio? How can you read what a choreographer wants, and how can you get in the creative zone? Our dancers have a few ideas...

Be prepared. There's no time to explain the whole ballet, you have to do a lot of learning yourself and come to the studio ready to show it. Know the steps, research the character, prepare your stamina, make sure your body's in good check. **Matthew Golding**

Every choreographer wants different things from you, so it's about reading that and morphing yourself into it. **Darcey Bussell**

It's communication. That's not talked about much and it's a skill that people forget is so vital. **Lauren Cuthbertson**

I really enjoy creative dancers. Yes, I give them the movement, but how do they *do* this movement? You don't want to be like a soldier, a robot. To really try to connect to the mindset of a choreographer is really exciting. It's very slippery to get this with words, it's like 'biting' the energy. **Hofesh Shechter**

It takes time to build up trust with a choreographer, but having something created on you is one of the best feelings ever. I go in like a bull in a china shop. They say jump and I try to jump as high as I can. **Steven McRae**

You want dancers to be smart enough to understand what's being required of them in the moment. If you're in a collaborative environment, you want dancers who are game and willing to give it a go and full of enthusiasm and ideas. If you're in a non-collaborative environment, a dancer's place is almost to be seen and not heard. **Kate Prince**

There is a certain amount of collaboration, of course. And if they ask you to give back, then you do that. But I think a lot of dancers get into problems because they don't agree with what the choreographer wants. But you have to remember that your role is to do what they want. You're not entitled to fight against their will. **Melissa Hamilton**

I would like a dancer to have no expectation of what I'm going to bring. You're able to interact with me, ask questions, try to find the detail. And be prepared to just move. Take the language of the movement and make it happen. Come with the right attitude, ready to have some fun, to work, to bring fire. **Kenrick Sandy**

Ask questions, definitely, but sometimes accept what you're being asked to do. Often I think choreographers don't know what they're talking about until they've seen it. I remember [dancer] Miguel Altunaga at Rambert used to say, 'It's not about you.' And quite often it isn't about you, it's about something bigger than you. The choreographer might be thinking globally and you're thinking more specifically. **Jonathan Goddard**

It's tentative when you start a new piece and you're starting from scratch. It's not about you trying to please the choreographer, it's about them testing out on you what they might want to see. Once you let that insecurity go, you're just a model for them to test things out and I think it's a bit easier. **Lauren Cuthbertson**

You have to do the steps in a way that's so natural it's like you're speaking through the steps. You have to learn the choreography so it's easy, and the timing. And then you have to play with it, you have to make it your own. Work out how can you feel comfortable when you're doing these steps as well as showing what the choreographer wants. **Matthew Golding**

You've got to go in completely open-minded. It's a case of going in and doing exactly what they ask, even if you don't like it. Just go for it and you might grow to like it. **Matthew Rees**

A creation has to evolve. What you experience on day one, most of the time, is nothing like it turns out in the end. I've learned over the years to try to be as open as I can with choreographers. Even if I feel it's not going to work and it's like watching a car crash, I still try to go into it head-first. They could have this vision that I haven't seen yet. **Steven McRae**

Don't be scared to make a mistake or think that there's a right or wrong answer. Collaboration is about ideas. Don't take it personally if your idea doesn't get chosen. When you're collaborating like that, a hundred things will get thrown in the pot and twenty will be saved. **Kate Prince**

Feeling creative is something you can't really demand. If you're having a good day, then it's amazing, and then you have days where you're completely stuck. You can spend a whole day doing a couple of eights. It's definitely a mindset thing. Listening to the right music can help. Something that has a memory attached to it, a time when you felt good or powerful or creative, something that has a good emotion attached to it. It's about getting good vibrations again. **Tommy Franzén**

Don't put up with crap. Don't let people speak to you like rubbish. You're not just a tool, where the choreographer says to jump on your head and you do it. You need to have a voice, but remember we're all trying to achieve something together here. **Steven McRae**

You need to be open to a choreographer, but I don't think you need to revere a choreographer too much. They need you as much as you need them. **Jonathan Goddard**

Getting into Character

Whether you aspire to be a swan-like Odile, a dramatic Carmen or a sassy Roxie Hart, the steps are just the start of it. If you take on character roles, you have to be able to act. Great dancers can disappear into their characters, so how do you learn to do that? Where do you find inspiration? Should you learn acting techniques as well as dance? And how do you bring a fresh slant to a classic role that's been danced many times?

To build a character, ask: who, where, why, when? It doesn't have to be one-dimensional, even with all of those fairytale stories. You can translate them into real life. **Teneisha Bonner**

With any role, the research you do will add to your interpretation. When I danced *Winter Dreams*, which was based on Chekhov's *Three Sisters*, it was seeing the play, watching the actresses and what they were feeling, reading the text, researching the era. Then with the choreographer, as soon as you've learned the moves, go away and try to bring something else into them. **Darcey Bussell**

One of my favourite characters to do is Mary Vetsera in *Mayerling*, because she was a real human being, and I enjoyed going into archives, investigating her life, researching her suicide and the historic context. All those things are so important. It doesn't mean that while you're dancing you have to have them in your head, but it creates a layer of knowledge so that this role becomes full, it becomes a whole person, rather than certain characteristics of a person. **Tamara Rojo**

Juliet's quite a hard one. She's not in Act Two of the ballet, apart from one small wedding scene, so I've learnt to always have the book with me and make sure I read again what's just happened on stage, and read what's coming so that I stay in the right place. Also in the ballet you don't see Juliet finding out that her cousin's been killed, so you have to go through that in your head before you end up in the next scene, otherwise you don't get to the depth that you could. **Lauren Cuthbertson**

I try and do all the research in terms of history, but I sometimes think it can be quite hindering to be too 'in your head' about it. There needs to be a real humanity, and that comes from me, not from textbooks. **Seeta Patel**

As a starting point, you have to see what the choreographer intended. Then you see how much a role has evolved with all the other dancers who've done it. Then you go in a different direction and try to bring something original that shakes people's predictions of the role. **Carlos Acosta**

When I danced *Manon*, I read the book, I watched films of different artists who had danced it before, and then I stopped watching anybody else and found my own way. I would try what someone else was doing and it would look horrendous – that's the problem if you try to imitate what's gone before. You have to trust yourself. Get in the studio on your own and record yourself and see what you like. **Melissa Hamilton**

When I go into a rehearsal room, I always say, 'Tell me what that moment is about? What are you thinking? What are you feeling? Why do you feel that way and how do you think the person next to you is feeling? And how do you feel about them?' Just try to build it up. Dancing shouldn't be one-dimensional. **Kate Prince**

Try to find an association that's going to help you create a character. For *Dracula*, I thought, what do I have in me that I could bring out in Dracula? And it was the idea that he's been around for so long, he's absolutely knackered! It made me think of the tiredness of dancing. How I feel when I'm really knackered from dancing, when I've done a tour and I'm completely drained of everything, but you just keep going; a steely, hard shell. **Jonathan Goddard**

Try to be natural and take your time. Pausing is a huge thing with acting, pausing and timing. **Matthew Golding**

Different roles command a different stance on stage. There are minor details. If I were a prince, I would walk toe-heel. Other characters, I'd walk heel-toe. If I were a prince, I wouldn't naturally go up to someone and shake their hand, I would stand and acknowledge them. People definitely wouldn't come up to you and touch you. If someone comes up to you in a stage rehearsal I'm like, 'Guys, back off, I'm a prince.' **Steven McRae**

I try to get closer to the real character. I don't want people to see me, I want them to see Prince Rudolf – with his look, his mannerisms – so you don't see Carlos Acosta. I'm not interested in just showing myself with a different outfit. **Carlos Acosta**

The first time I did Romeo, I only had five days to prepare it. I remember Monica Mason, my director at the time, said, 'Be yourself. Don't try to be anything else.' I was a young man, Romeo is a young man. He's fallen in love, I was in love. And I still try to hold on to that every time I go back to it. But as I get older and my life changes, I hope that every time I revisit it, I'm able to create more layers. Over the years, I've encountered a lot of different emotions, so you try to put that back into your art. **Steven McRae**

Part and parcel of doing musicals is that you have to play characters. If you don't know how to, or you don't have an instinct to, you're going to fall behind. My personal interest is physical comedy and mime, creating a story with your body. Musical theatre is about being a clown most of the time. I'm a complete ham, but I've never enjoyed ham acting – even the best clown, although they're completely over the top, you believe them. **Adam Garcia**

It can be as much about being a comedian as it is about being emotive. I think the girls struggle with it more. Girls hit puberty at a crucial point in dance training and they become self-conscious. Boys, on the other hand, just want to show off. I've had to work really hard with our young girls to put two fingers up to the boys and say, 'I can be as big a character as you.' **Kate Prince**

I love roles where I can almost use it as therapy, where I can release a part of myself. It can feel safe because you get to release so much emotion, it can be very truthful. If you can touch people with it, that's the most important thing. People go to the theatre to experience something and to be touched. **Melissa Hamilton**

It just takes a little bit of intelligence, to feel, to have a little story in your head, to be trying to express something, even if it's just, 'I had a bad day and I feel really bad about myself and I'm going to make this dance to offload it' or if it's your rebellion or about how small someone made you feel. **Kate Prince**

I don't excessively research. In terms of watching previous dancers do roles, I don't do it. It would be like putting on someone else's jacket each time. I definitely try to *be* the character, but in order to make it realistic there has to be a bit of you in there. Otherwise it's just a cardboard cut-out of what I think Romeo should be. There's still got to be an element of Steven in there. **Steven McRae**

I don't like to over-rehearse, because I don't think senti-ments should be over-rehearsed. There should be an understanding of the arc of the story. In Bharata Natyam metaphor is used a lot. You have the line of song, which has a direct word-to-word meaning, and you start off describing it, but then the metaphors develop around that. You build the intensity. In order for there to be a cli-max you can't give everything away at the beginning. **Seeta Patel**

You just have to imagine how that character would act, in their whole being. Not just relying on the steps to tell the story. In that way, you can bring something to the smallest in-between steps and gestures – they suddenly mean volumes. When I watch ballet that doesn't have those links, as a member of the audience I'm just not transported. **Lauren Cuthbertson**

I'm not interested in an illusion of emotion; I don't want to project an idea of love. No, for me, you have to *be* in love with me. I have to live on stage. It's just you and me, and when you get that chemistry it's wonderful. Some people are very good at projecting an image of some-thing, but you know when it's fake. **Carlos Acosta**

For a while I really believed in the Method style of performance, that dramatic school. I manipulated my own emotions. And although you do deliver quite an emotional performance, I'm not sure they are the best performances I've given. I think I've gone back to the more British system of acting, which is a mixture of using your emotions, but more importantly, using your intellect. For the Method, you put yourself in situations that you don't really need to. It becomes very self-indulgent. **Tamara Rojo**

Even the stuff that we do that's abstract is still character-based. Even if what we're trying to convey to an audience is just a feeling, it has to be more than the steps. Dance is an expression, so you should be expressing something, not just expressing how high you can kick your leg. **Kate Prince**

Tips on Partnering

Fonteyn and Nureyev; Fred and Ginger – whether in ballet or ballroom, often the spotlight is shared and great partnerships can go down in history. Is it natural chemistry or just practice? The dancers share some tips on how to find harmony with your onstage 'other half'.

First of all you need to be ready for whoever you're dancing with. I do my push-ups, I'm ready, no one's going to blow me away. I'm going to be there, solid, for them, and that takes work aside from the normal training. Be very attentive. Listen to what your partner needs, because everybody's body is different. The other thing is being the complement to her fragility and femininity. These two poles [male and female] are very defined. **Carlos Acosta**

To be a good partner, be a good listener. Don't say much, just listen and understand that everyone wants to do their best. I would say for the guys: it's always your fault. In the sense that when something happens, whatever the woman does, you have the ability to fix it. You have to be completely in the moment and aware, flexible and changing. **Matthew Golding**

If I'm partnering, I want the ballerina to be happy. The moments that I've been on stage with ballerinas and it just feels right are incredible, and that's something rare to find. With some people you can never quite understand how to partner them. But that is like relationships in life.

You don't get on with every single person, not every partnership fits like a glove. But I think if two dancers are professional enough they can work out a happy medium. **Steven McRae**

You have to be quite diplomatic. If something isn't working, you don't want them to think you're blaming them. It might be you. You need to ask, 'Is there anything I can do to help you with that?' You just have to be kind to them and they'll be kind back. But sometimes a bit of friction adds to it, someone you have a bit of feistiness with. That can be a good mix: you almost go out to prove each other wrong. **Lauren Cuthbertson**

It's always good to understand what the woman's steps are. Understand what she's dancing and think what you would want to feel if you were doing that. You're actually dancing her steps with your hands. Close your eyes and don't look at where the girl is, it's all in the hands. **Matthew Golding**

Steven McRae

5

On Stage

Pre-show Rituals

Showtime is approaching and preparation is key. The dancers talk about warming up, costumes and make-up, getting into the right head space, and transforming into character.

Pre-show rituals are all part of the show. Setting out your costumes, getting your make-up and hair done – it is all the process of the show. Once you're in that theatre, you're at work, and it has a structure and I love that structure, it's so exciting. **Aaron Sillis**

I give myself time before the show. I will always be there about four hours before the show, doing my make-up, doing my hair. That's always part of the transformation. I always feel that with make-up, you first erase yourself, and then you start building the character. So that's all part of the process. **Tamara Rojo**

I'm rubbish at make-up. If you're a principal you get your hair and make-up done for you, which I loved, because I was so bad at it. It's different on a video shoot, it's really heavily airbrushed, but on stage you need to get the contouring right. **Aaron Sillis**

I've had costumes I'm uncomfortable with and I've gone discreetly to the choreographer or the costume department and said, 'Can I have a little bit of something to cover here,' and more often than not they've been really lovely about it. As I've got older I've tried to know a little bit more about who I'm auditioning for. I'm totally comfortable with my body, but I don't want to do something with a lack of integrity. **Teneisha Bonner**

Always go to do warm-ups, even if you've done a class in the day. Always do that company warm-up before the show. If it doesn't warm you up, then get there early and do your own thing. But be part of the company. **Stephen Mear**

We always do warm-up together in the studio. It brings everyone together. When everyone comes in, doing stretches, chatting, the energy is all over the place. But once you start warming up that's when the energy comes together, in unison. **Tommy Franzén**

We have a focus exercise we do: right foot, left foot, stamp in a circle. That's just to break the ice and get everyone on the same page and the same unified front. **Kenrick Sandy**

Try to avoid superstitions. The only thing that matters to me on a show day is waking up and being the right temperature. I don't mean literally the right temperature, I mean a nice emotional state, where I feel very in control and free and calm. When I was younger, I didn't want to talk to my family on the day because they might say the wrong thing and push me over the edge. Now, they can say anything to me, as long as I am in control of myself. I take responsibility for that. If having that planned routine gives you confidence then that's great, but I found that it made me feel quite restricted. **Lauren Cuthbertson**

There's supposed to be a two-hour break before the performance, and I eat right at the beginning of that break, and then I sleep. We used to do it at Rambert, you'd put the yoga mats out. You work so hard, I remember the pleasure of just laying on the floor. It was so intense not to move. If I can sleep for forty-five minutes, then I'll do a floor barre, and then go through anything I'm worried about, and then go out and perform. **Jonathan Goddard**

Dancers now change roles all the time. You move from one contemporary abstract work to a full-on love story. You really have to focus and it's very much about creating the mood. Listen to the music of the ballet while you're warming up. You often just need a quiet space, not to be around too many people. I did breathing exercises in the wings before I would make each entrance and that would calm my heart rate. **Darcey Bussell**

In the time leading up to a show, I start thinking about the character's intention, his background, and keep my mind in that space. When I'm starting a new show it takes a bit longer, but then it becomes more and more automatic, you snap into it. In my last show, *The Five & the Prophecy of Prana* [Franzén played a martial-arts master], I would listen to Chinese music, watch t'ai chi and get myself into the zone. I *am* this master. **Tommy Franzén**

There's this internal scream that I tend to do before I go on stage. It's a roar that I do, then I go straight out and perform. **Kenrick Sandy**

Dealing with Nerves

Your heart's pounding, your palms are sweating, a faint feeling of nausea is rising and suddenly you can't remember the steps... Nerves can be a minor annoyance or a major hindrance, but you're unlikely to get away with never feeling them. Can you turn 'bad' nerves into 'good'? Does it help to have a pre-show ritual? If you're worried about stage fright and palpitations, our dancers are here to help, and to tell you why getting naked might be the answer...

Nerves are healthy, everyone gets it. *Britain's Got Talent* was scary – being in front of Simon Cowell is enough. But it's how you embrace it once you get on stage. We have a team talk and team prayers and we're motivating each other and psyching each other up and really keeping that togetherness, because we're going out there as a team. That's the benefit of having a group. When you're going out there on your own it's different, you really need to have a focus. **Marlon Wallen**

Nerves are a very good thing. If you don't have nerves there's a problem. When I was doing *Dorian Gray* at Sadler's Wells I was nearly sick with nerves, pre-, during and post-show. Waiting to go on in the wings, I would be panicking, for the whole two-week run, because I cared so much about doing it right. But for me, dance is that escape, so when I'm on stage, everything else disappears and it's just me in my element. **Aaron Sillis**

I actually felt worse if I wasn't nervous. It was a way of focusing and realising where I really was. If I was relaxed about a role I'd feel that I wasn't going to get into it and that would upset me. So any sort of edge you can bring to it, I loved. Of course, as soon as the music starts and you're in it, suddenly the nerves disappear anyway. **Darcey Bussell**

There's a fear of disappointing people, a fear of not being good enough. That's when it will come and play games with your mind and that's when I've found that having rituals, having a consistent way of preparing for something, for me, is the only way not to succumb to panic. **Tamara Rojo**

I've been so nervous I've vomited before a show. It affects your singing, it affects your dancing. The tension affects my tapping. I've no idea how to stop it. Hypnosis – does that work? **Adam Garcia**

I'd never done anything nude before. It was a very brief scene and I felt no qualms about it, but it wasn't until the tech rehearsal that I had to do it. I remember the first time, my heart was beating so quickly, but as soon as I'd flashed, everything else disappeared and it was so freeing. Then I would always look forward to it, because whatever nerves I had would dissipate for the rest of the show. **Aaron Sillis**

Obviously you get anxious about performances, because you have expectations, but take a bit of the pressure off yourself. If you know you've genuinely worked your butt off and you've put the work in, you have to trust yourself that you're going to go on there and do the best you possibly can at that point in time. **Steven McRae**

Turn the nerves into something good. Some people might dance around, jump up and down, have a bit of fun, joke around. Some people might meditate, take some deep breaths and get the heart rate down. **Tommy Franzén**

I don't think nerves go away. Just give yourself as much preparation as you can. If you still can't quite control it, go and ask for help. There are plenty of sports psychologists that can help you with practical steps that can get you in a good frame of mind. There's nothing wrong with asking for psychological help. **Tamara Rojo**

Lack of confidence and being nervous certainly shuts down your ability to be in the moment. You have to find your own way of freeing yourself up, whether that be in a room by yourself or with friends, or at a club or a festival; somewhere you feel you can do whatever you want and express yourself however you want. **Adam Garcia**

In the wings, this is the moment that you've been waiting for. Eight hours every day is all for this. So you might as well enjoy it. Finally: lights, camera, action! It's a unique moment in time, never going to be repeated again. The minute that you begin living it, everything disappears. You're in the moment, it's wonderful. **Carlos Acosta**

Taking the Spotlight

The curtain goes up, you hear your cue and you step out on stage. Now what? What makes a good performance great? How can you make the most of that time on stage? Should you be thinking about the audience, or not?

I like to show off to an audience. I want to impress them. I guess that's the first part of audience engagement. It's like a date. It's like seduction. You meet each other and then you've got to charm them. And then they'll really like you, whatever you do. **Adam Garcia**

When I get on stage, I'm not Kenrick Sandy, I am my alter ego, H2O. That character has a different kind of energy. Where Kenrick may be tired from the day, as soon as I get on stage it's H2O. Most dancers in hip hop do that, have an aka. It helps you energise yourself for the performance. As an individual you can feel quite vulnerable sometimes, so it's best to put out someone who is more confident and outgoing, so the real you can just be happy and cool. **Kenrick Sandy**

On stage, you automatically have to turn yourself into an entertainer. You're no longer dancing for yourself, there's an audience, they need to be entertained, that's what you're there to do. You can afford to be charismatic, cocky; you can afford to be a little bit cheeky, because now you're entertaining, it won't come across as arrogant. **Marlon Wallen**

I think of the audience as a dreamlike void. It's not like I'm selling it to individual people in the audience. I don't kick it out, unless the piece demands that. The way I think of it is like a big black mirror that's quite far away, so you're looking towards what is essentially yourself, in a loop. Also, I don't wear contacts, and that really helps. If I don't have my glasses on it helps me to internalise. **Jonathan Goddard**

Generally I'm aware the audience is there, but I don't really think about that. When the curtain goes up and you see a mass of people it's horribly scary, but once you've done it a few times it becomes the norm. **Aaron Sillis**

I love being on stage. I just like to mess with the audience's heads sometimes. I pull them in, take them back. It's how you look at them, your focus. **Kenrick Sandy**

On stage it's just being in the zone. If you're playing a character, just be really focused and into it. I think of filling the space, being as wide as possible in all three dimensions when I dance, with my presence but also physically. Take as much space as possible. And attention. Demand attention. **Tommy Franzén**

Look at the volume of where you're performing and how far the audience are away from you and make your performance relative to that. If I'm performing in immersive theatre I might be right next to you – I try to make a human connection in the performance. The space and the performance should be relative. **Jonathan Goddard**

When I'm performing, my world is the stage and the dancers on the stage. Although I'm performing to the audience, I'm also performing to the dancers on the stage. It's three hundred and sixty degrees. When you've got your set and your costume and you're in character, it's a world of your own. And it's really nice that other people are witnessing that, but it's also very private. **Aaron Sillis**

The one thing I'd always think about was what my coach had said to me from one step to the next. It would be this kind of wheel going on in my mind, rolling out the script of what I've got to do, always thinking. There would only be roles like Juliet and Manon where you could sometimes forget about the technique and get carried away with the role. **Darcey Bussell**

I like to give the cast a word before each show. You might use a word like 'ignite', so in everything you're doing you're igniting every moment. I did it for *The Metamorphosis*. 'Today go for *Kafkaesque*. Today it's about the mother.' It helps the dancers find something different. As a performer, keep discovering. Even though you think you might know something, there's always something new to find and to make better. **Arthur Pita**

For battling, sometimes the only way to know how it feels is to be in it. There aren't necessarily dos and don'ts when it comes to battling. You have to learn your technique, your foundation, but when you're in that ring and the music takes you, the music takes you. There's nothing you can really do. **Kenrick Sandy**

When you freestyle, you go into a form of trance. For me, when a freestyle's coming up, I easily start going into combinations and tricks I want to fit in. But it works best when I just open myself to whatever happens at that moment. Just let the music come up and guide you, flow through you; you and the music in a duet. That's when the most beautiful things come out, in complete openness and harmony with the music. **Tommy Franzén**

The minute I accepted that no performance is going to be perfect, I started to enjoy it much more. Those moments when you feel something click and it feels right, even if it lasts thirty seconds – those are the moments that I hold on to when I walk off stage. Then the next morning, when you go back to class and you put your hand on the barre, you think, 'Okay, how can I improve that?' It's a debriefing. **Steven McRae**

Beyond the Theatre

There are many jobs for dancers beyond the theatre. It might be going on a global stadium tour with a pop megastar, making a music video, or appearing in a dance movie or on TV, and every medium has its own demands and expectations. The dancers share their know-how on working in the commercial world, and reveal whether going on tour with Kylie is as glamorous as you'd think.

In theatre you're getting into a character, working with other performers and having a narrative for the audience to understand. You get something completely different out of pop. When I did the Take That tour we had 80,000 people in a stadium and it's an insane, euphoric release. The adrenalin rush is completely different. **Aaron Sillis**

I worked with Kylie on her X tour in South America. And then I did the Progress tour for Take That. Is it as fun as you'd imagine? Abso-freakin'-lutely! You're working for these people on big-budget projects, you get treated really well. It's epic. They were both an absolute joy to work for. I grew up not being bothered about Take That, but there I was at the side of the stage singing 'Never Forget', just loving life. **Teneisha Bonner**

When you're dancing in pop it's about being very clean and executing exactly the same movement, usually in unison. You can't be a soloist, you have to fit into a group of people. You're not allowed as much artistic flair. Some performers aren't good at working in the pop world because they stand out too much. If you get a chance for a solo, then you can push it forward, but when you're in a group you have to pull it back. **Aaron Sillis**

Stadium gigs are brilliant. The vibe is great, performing to that many people. That said, I don't like it as much as the theatre, because you don't have that connection with the audience. In a stadium you're looking out on a sea of people and they look like ants. There's so many of them it's overwhelming, but they're not there for you. They're there for the artists and you're propping up the artists. You're a small bit of the puzzle. **Teneisha Bonner**

In pop videos it's 'camera-face' at the ready. I hate to say it, and it depends on the project, but with a lot of pop videos it's about looking very sexy. It's that pouted expression, staring into the distance. You have to retain this air of sexy mystery. It's really naff. **Aaron Sillis**

On film, the camera soaks up so much of your energy, so you have to give ten times more on film for it to look like anything. You really have to go at it, making sure your lines are clearer and sharper, especially when you start getting tired. It's easier to cover that on stage. On film, because the camera saps your energy anyway, you look tired. **Teneisha Bonner**

I'd advise any dancer looking to go into dance films to get your acting up. The last one that I did was *StreetDance 3D* and we had to train actors how to dance. My argument would be, why don't we teach dancers how to act? Come on, dancers, you need to learn how to act, how to project and animate yourself in front of a camera. **Kenrick Sandy**

For TV, you have to remember that the TV world has a certain vision of what they want when it comes to their viewers, they know their audience. They know what they want from each show so you have to be versatile. It's not the same as doing your own show. **Marlon Wallen**

Making Mistakes

Wardrobe malfunctions, mind-blanks, missed cues and dropped props, falling out of your pirouette or tripping over the scenery. All these things can, and do, happen. That's the magic of live theatre, they say. That's also the humiliation of messing up in front of hundreds of people. Think it doesn't happen to the pros? Our dancers know otherwise.

I have this ability to suddenly do the wrong step and then everything unravels. The last time was two weeks ago. Don't worry about it, style it out. And listen to the music – it's like somebody telling you what the steps are, like having a feed in your ear. One time I lay on the floor during a duet until I recognised something in the music. The person I was doing the duet with obviously suddenly didn't have their partner, so they just started improvising. **Jonathan Goddard**

It's both the horrible thing about theatre and the beauty of it: you can have a horrific moment where you want the stage to swallow you up, feeling humiliated and the curtain comes down and you feel shit. And then the next night it's a completely new audience that have never seen the show before and you get to make amends. **Adam Garcia**

Anything could go wrong on stage, and when it happens, everything goes into slow motion. I had a crazy moment where my partner's legs cramped up and she couldn't move at all. I just carried her around the stage. We kept going. Half the audience knew something funny was going on, but some didn't realise. I started adding jumps and changing the choreography and at the end we said: 'Phew, we really experienced that one.' **Matthew Golding**

There was a youth competition in New York and my teacher decided to throw me in at the deep end. It was sink or swim. I drowned totally. I was eighteen and I had no idea what being on stage felt like. I completely messed up my variation. I landed practically flat on the floor in the final and yet I came away with the Grand Prix. In my eyes I had totally failed, but I was being rewarded for it. What I had shown was potential. **Melissa Hamilton**

Even if you fall over, just totally act like you meant to do that. It's like walking down the street when you trip on the kerb. Just carry on. You forget about it two blocks along the road. **Steven McRae**

I think the advice would always be to say that there's no perfect performance. There will always be something you're not happy with, and for a young dancer, accepting that is important. You will make mistakes, you will fall over or hit the scenery, or each other. It can seem a great tragedy, there are tears, but know that it doesn't matter. Carry on, get on with it. **Matthew Bourne**

Even if you're doing the wrong thing, as long as you're convincing, as long as you have conviction, maybe they'll think, 'Oh, everyone else is wrong.' Keep selling it. **Adam Garcia**

If it goes wrong, just go with it. I would always go with it rather than trying to cover it up. When it happens, it happens. Embrace it. 'Wrong and strong' is what Kate Prince usually says. **Tommy Franzén**

It's so easy to come off stage and think, 'Goddammit, I messed up that turn.' The adrenalin is pumping, you're so angry at yourself – or someone else. But dancers are very quick at writing off that whole show. Okay, so it wasn't perfect, but that's why people come to live theatre. If someone falls over, they get the biggest applause. People like to be wowed, but they also like to see that you're human. **Steven McRae**

For a long time I used ballet as a way to validate myself. So if I did well, then I felt good. If I did badly, I felt horrendous, I would crumble. I've now got to the point where I don't validate myself through ballet and it's a lot easier to cope. **Melissa Hamilton**

People have said to me: 'Aren't you the guy who fell over?' The last part of *Tap Dogs* is an encore on narrow steel girders. Lo and behold, I slipped and fell off the stage and landed on the front row. All the reviewers were in. I don't know why, but I stood back up and curtsied. And it was reviewed: 'He fell off and did a curtsy and then got up and did it again, and it was great.' Yeah, you're going to fall over every now and again. David Beckham missed a penalty in the World Cup and he's doing all right. **Adam Garcia**

What Makes a Great Dancer?

Everyone aspires to be the sort of dancer that you can't take your eyes off; the dancer everyone talks about after the show. But what do we really mean when we talk about the 'x factor'? Can you teach charisma, or is it just the case that you either have it, or you don't? The dancers share some ideas on what makes an artist great.

I think a dancer needs to have curiosity and discipline. **Seeta Patel**

I'd say a dancer shows you the step and an artist makes you *feel* the step. **Melissa Hamilton**

Virtuosity is really important, but I would take someone who could do a few less spins but was really going to entertain me. I'd go for performance every time. **Kate Prince**

The best dancers are intelligent dancers. They have an understanding of their own bodies, of storytelling and expression, and a very keen eye. They have an ability to use their bodies expressively and can really explore different moods and different ways of moving. I think extraordinary dancers are really quite rare. There are many brilliant technical dancers, but those who have that extra way of expressing something are the ones that draw my eye. **Arlene Phillips**

I think it's a musicality, a response to the music. And it's the way they interact with their fellow dancers on stage. A lot of people can get into doing the part for themselves and forget that it's an ensemble. Once you're out there you only have each other. **Cassa Pancho**

Be a thinking dancer. You can go and do whatever you're told, that's easy. But I think developing an inner world of imagery or creativity is another thing. Translating the orders that you get from a teacher in an interesting way; finding an image or a thought that is connected to a sensation. It's being really creative with the way that you access your body. **Hofesh Shechter**

I know a lot of great dancers who I won't work with because they don't make me feel anything. They don't engage me. I don't mind watching them from a distance, I can appreciate their skill, but their performance is the thing that would hook me in. **Kate Prince**

Be musical. For me, it's catastrophic not being on the music. The movement should be an extension of the music. **Carlos Acosta**

There's a difference between a dancer and a performer. A dancer knows the moves, you understand 'five, six, seven, eight...' Then it's about really projecting, animating and showcasing yourself – that's a performer. By adding characterisation, intention, feeling, you start to take it to another level and be more creative and innovative – that's an artist. If you create a brand, that's celebrity. And by the time you've reached your peak and people want to do a case study of you, that's a legend. **Kenrick Sandy**

This is a personal opinion but maybe a touch of anarchy or self-possession is great in a dancer. So you take the material you're doing as seriously as you possibly can, but within that you look for your own interpretation, so you're in control and you're playing with it and you're communicating it. **Jonathan Goddard**

Dance, at the end of the day, is all about us feeling things when we're watching it. When you look at a dancer performing, you are looking to have an experience, to be excited, thrilled, moved. It's an ancient thing. Through the dancer you experience life in an enhanced way. To convey emotion you need to feel emotion. A dancer has to experience something. If he doesn't experience something, nobody will. **Hofesh Shechter**

There isn't one right way to be a dancer. Look at all the stars around the world – how can you say one way is the right way? We're all trying to aim for what is correct and what is right, but there's no right or wrong answer. We're all striving for something that doesn't even exist in the first place. **Melissa Hamilton**

Ultimately it's that spark that you're looking for, that passion. When people display a passion for what they're doing it really draws you in. Even if there are flaws. **Matthew Bourne**

I don't think you can teach dancers to dance from the soul. That has to come from you. **Stephen Mear**

I've been doing movement direction in theatre and I was surprised by how long it takes for actors to understand the meaning of what they're saying and communicate it. And I think that's the same for dancers. An actor has to internalise the text and understand it and then they apply technique, and then they start to communicate. They're talking *to* someone, and in dance you have to think you're talking to someone too. **Jonathan Goddard**

Charisma? I think it's just good lighting, good make-up. **Matthew Golding**

Stage presence is something you can learn. Certainly experience gives you it, because you're more confident, more comfortable on stage; you're very at home in your body and in who you are and that becomes very appealing, people who seem very natural in their reactions. **Matthew Bourne**

It's about getting totally comfortable in your own skin and being at home with yourself. **Teneisha Bonner**

Even in an abstract work, why are you drawn to one dancer more than another? Because they seem to be investing the movement with something, and I think that's bringing themselves to it and not putting on a fake persona. So many dancers have a fakey dance face – happy, sad, tragic – and you can feel it's just plastered on. **Matthew Bourne**

For me, dancers that think they've 'got it' are kind of boring. In our art form there is no indication of whether what you're doing is right or wrong. It's only cultural agreement. So the idea that somebody feels like they're doing it really well, for me that doesn't work. But the idea that there are a million ways of doing it and somebody did it in an interesting way, now that I can accept. It's the endless search. **Hofesh Shechter**

6

Choreography

Kenrick 'H2O' Sandy

Becoming a Choreographer

There are many different routes to becoming a choreographer. Some are former dancers who turn to making their own work once their performing careers are over, others have always known they wanted to be the one in charge. If you want to create your own work – rather than dance other people's – where on earth do you start? Some of the UK's top choreographers, whose work is now seen around the globe, take us back to the beginning.

For me, choreography was always there from the word go. I was always the one who wanted to put the show on, I wanted to do a number. I always had the instinct for running a company, I always wanted to bring people together and call it something, give it a name. **Matthew Bourne**

Just do it. You don't need anything. I've been telling people I was a choreographer since I was a kid. The first piece of work I ever choreographed on stage, I was eight or nine, and I had three girls in my school and we put together a routine to 'Big in Japan'. If it's in you, it's in you. I remember meeting strangers and saying, 'I'm a choreographer,' way before anybody had ever paid me to be one. **Kate Prince**

Making choreography is not something you do after you dance, when your dance career is over. For me, the practice of being creative and making things, you could be doing from seven or eight years old. **Wayne McGregor**

Everyone has ideas. But it's making them happen that is the hard work. You talk to a lot of dancers, they say, 'I have an idea for a piece I want to make.' Well, execute that. What's your plan to make it happen? You see them later, 'Oh, it never really happened, I didn't get any support.' No, you just have to try and make it happen. **Arthur Pita**

I think there are different reasons people want to do choreography. Some people may enjoy the idea of giving a bow at the end of a show, or the idea that maybe they will be successful, or they will be an artist. But actually making choreography is a lot more than those things. Most of your life is in the studio, or in administration. Make sure you want to do it, because there's a lot of shit involved. **Hofesh Shechter**

Before I'd even started my university course I went to the freshers' fair, joined the amateur dramatics society and got the job of choreographer on the first musical. I was going round hair salons and saying I was a choreographer and do you do hair shows, do you need somebody to choreograph your hair show? **Kate Prince**

It was really out of frustration that I started Hot Gossip. I would go out and dance in clubs and it seemed to me to have no relationship to the dance I was seeing on television – step, kick and smile! So I took the best dancers from my class, who were a real motley bunch because they were the ones who didn't look 'right' for TV. I myself was rejected, I was short and stocky and quite a tough dancer. It certainly changed my life. **Arlene Phillips**

I remember one of our ballet masters at the beginning would say, 'Oh, we're trying to start a company.' And that would really annoy me, because I thought, 'We *have* a company.' It may not be great, yet, but we've got one, so let's not be apologetic about it. Let's take ownership of it. **Cassa Pancho**

The way the dance industry works, the better a dancer you are, the easier your transition into the world of choreography. If you don't have a reputation as a great dancer, it's much harder to be considered to be a good or great or innovative choreographer, and that's always been an interesting challenge for me. **Maxine Doyle**

Choreographers don't necessarily have to be great dancers. I think sometimes we get fooled into thinking that great dancers will become great choreographers or great directors, but they're completely different things. A dance training is necessary, but there's a lot more about dance you can learn as well as technique – dance history, criticism, movement study – and you have to watch a lot, of course. **Matthew Bourne**

For some people, having a formalised dance education is very engaging, but often it can be a very conceptual process. For others it's just about getting dancers – their friends usually – in a room and trying things out and seeing what happens. Sometimes when people go to university, the passion is in some way edited out, but others find it hard to progress without an organised curriculum and structure, so it really depends on your personality. **Wayne McGregor**

The first ten years I did as many workshops as I could. I did a lot of training, courses in dance, theatre, anything I thought I might get something out of. I was always applying for anything I could get funding or sponsorship for. **Maxine Doyle**

One of the useful things for me about university was my whole engagement with semiotics and the Bauhaus, opening up my ideas about the ways that things are organised and made. Going to university is not just about going to do dance, it's the other connections you can make while you're there. **Wayne McGregor**

Watch everything: plays, musicals, exhibitions. Just indulge in everything as much as you can. Go and see other people's work and learn from it. Be in the scene. **Arthur Pita**

One of the things I'm asked most by choreographers is how to get into musical theatre. You have to become either an assistant or an associate to someone working in musical theatre to get into that world. Often you could have a lucrative career doing a hair show or a design show or a music video, but you have to give that up to spend a year assisting on a musical in order to get into that world. **Arlene Phillips**

While I was in shows I became dance captain, looking after the show, so that can be the next step towards becoming a choreographer. **Stephen Mear**

I was a dance teacher at summer camp after I graduated and that was quite definitive for me. It was a performing-arts camp. I taught everything – jazz, ballet, Shakespeare, musical theatre. But the most exciting thing was that all the other tutors were practising young artists. On our nights off, we'd put the kids to bed and go to the studio and have these massive jams that would last all night. **Maxine Doyle**

When you start, the idea of structure is good – one you might follow, or break, but something to begin with. For me, it was: 'I have ten days, I'm going to go to the studio and make something.' That was the structure. It allows you a place to play. **Hofesh Shechter**

Your reputation can rest almost on one piece sometimes. That can see you through a whole career. It's about finding something that's going to capture the imagination of everyone early on. Do something that's going to make people remember you. Take a famous piece of music and do something with it that people don't expect, or a title that sticks in the mind. You can't expect people to know about you if you don't do something that makes them remember you. **Matthew Bourne**

Having a purpose is really good, like a show, a competition, a festival. Something you have to work for, so that you have to complete it. If it doesn't have boundaries, then it's not work, it's just practice. Otherwise you can fly forever and never form anything. **Hofesh Shechter**

It's got to come from an idea. What is it you want to share? You've got to think: 'Oh my god, I cannot go to the grave unless people experience this. I have to share this with you.' **Arthur Pita**

Honing Your Craft

Form and structure, emotion and storytelling, big intellectual ideas and mundane observations on everyday life – how do you wrest them all from the movement of human bodies? How do you communicate those ideas to an audience? How do you get better at what you do? Our choreographers explain.

When you walk into the studio, do whatever you feel like. Judge it afterwards. Do first, ask questions later. **Hofesh Shechter**

Get your basics down. Space and time. Space and time is what choreography is. And have something to say. **Arthur Pita**

To become a good choreographer you just have to do a lot of choreography. Take every opportunity, every company that asks you, every little thing, even if it feels difficult or stupid. The more you do it, the more you'll get better. It's pretty straightforward. **Hofesh Shechter**

You improve by doing. By making lots of mistakes. By trying not to repeat what you've done before. By borrowing ways of thinking from other domains and applying them to yours. It's about remaining curious and open, and being disciplined in how you work. I'm the sort of person who'll go into the studio and do my five or six hours a day, even if I don't feel like it. That discipline of just *doing* is a way of improving the craft. You're not waiting for divine inspiration to strike, it's a workmanlike attitude. **Wayne McGregor**

I know choreographers who go in the room and have the whole show set. I don't know how that works. I build it on the people I have with me and I will add anything in that makes them look brilliant. **Stephen Mear**

I think it's really important to be with dancers in real time, touching them, moving them, staying connected to your own body. Not standing back and only watching and losing touch with your own physical dimension. I think it's really important that you practise both. **Wayne McGregor**

Bringing dancers into the process is a good lesson. Don't think you've got to do everything yourself. You don't have to agree with everyone – you have the final say – but I think it's good to bring them into your confidence about what you're feeling, get them to explore similar things, send them home with something to watch or read, and the next day ask what they felt. The best pieces are sometimes when, at the end of it, you can't remember who said or made what. **Matthew Bourne**

Something brilliant that Sam Mendes said: choose your collaborators well. The good collaborators will be the ones that will debate with you and provoke you. Choose those people who will make you better. And use everyone's imagination. If you're working with a cast of twenty-five, that's twenty-five imaginations in the room. Don't think you've got to be totally in charge. **Arthur Pita**

Have a really good template of ideas, but then be completely open to smashing that structure apart, and working with the dancers you've got in the room and getting the best out of them. **Aaron Sillis**

I learn my music so well, like you wouldn't believe. I made myself learn to read music so I could have a drummer in and say, 'I want a jazz drum here, a hi-hat there,' so the drummer isn't rolling his eyes at you when you ask for a 'bang and a hit and a ting'. **Stephen Mear**

I remember doing a choreographic course with Bob Cohan and he said to always go into the room with an idea and always know how you're going to run your session. And I think that's excellent advice. It might be that all you know is you're going to try something with circles, but at least you have that. Maybe it does work for some people to have a blank canvas, but I remember being a dancer and working with people who had that method and feeling lost. **Arthur Pita**

Try different techniques. Throw some acting techniques into the dancing. Work with different structures of making. But you also need to have a strong vision of where you want to go and not get too distracted from that. **Aaron Sillis**

The first time I really felt I could believe in myself was when I was with DV8 and I saw Lloyd Newson do it. He would ask us for a bunch of opinions. He'd have the conversation and think about it, and then decide to do what he wanted to do in the first place anyway. Thinking is what's important. It's about knowing why you're doing the thing you're doing. **Seeta Patel**

Bring your own spice to the mix. **Kenrick Sandy**

Choreography for me is a lot about the game between letting something happen, letting yourself be a bit silly, and then forming it and making sense of it. It's a lot about controlling the energy in the studio – it's crowd control. I enjoy working with my dancers like friends. They know I'm their boss, but there's a very light-hearted atmosphere in the studio, and that allows us to snap into working really hard for an hour and then snap out of it. **Hofesh Shechter**

You have to sell it. It's about inspiring dancers and getting them to trust you. I always say to people, 'I will never make you look stupid, trust me.' **Stephen Mear**

The more space I have, the more ideas just come. It's not like I need seven weeks in the Bahamas, but it's making sure you wake up ten minutes earlier in the morning, or take an hour before rehearsal to go for a walk. Things happen in the mind when you're given the space. **Hofesh Shechter**

You can't make too many pieces. If you think of people like George Balanchine and Jerome Robbins, they were making every day. We've conflated this idea of funding, where funding only allows you to make a certain amount of pieces a year, with the need to make. And I think if you're a maker and you want to practise your craft, you have to be doing it all the time. **Wayne McGregor**

Some people would say you shouldn't care if there's an audience for your work, but I always did. I always wanted to make work for an audience, and not just an audience of dancers. **Maxine Doyle**

It's ultimately about audiences, or it should be. **Matthew Bourne**

In musical theatre your choreography has to be able to adapt to the storytelling and you have to be a good collaborator. You are rarely free to go off and do whatever you want. It's part of a bigger collaboration between the writers, the director, the designers, everyone. **Arlene Phillips**

Don't just throw loads of steps in to prove yourself. I had one of the best bits of advice from Julia McKenzie, who was directing *A Little Night Music* when I was starting off as a choreographer. She turned to me one day and said, 'Stephen, you are a brilliant choreographer, but just because you have a parasol in your hand, doesn't mean you have to twirl it.' Don't throw in the kitchen sink! **Stephen Mear**

Don't be afraid to work in a way that is not the 'professional' way. Because nobody knows what the professional way is. Whatever turns you on. **Hofesh Shechter**

Don't step on the laugh line. Don't choreograph while they're singing and dancing. Be careful that you're not doing a pirouette on the gag. I remember Victoria Wood saying to me, 'Stephen, you can't do that. You just stood on a laugh line.' You can't have someone doing a monologue and someone behind them doing trenches. You've got to know where your focus is. It's about directing the attention. **Stephen Mear**

What comes out is what's right in the moment. Sometimes it can be an advantage having to make really quick decisions. Go with it, just do something. **Aaron Sillis**

Have a notebook, or an iPhone, to capture your ideas. These ideas come and you think, 'That's such a good idea, of course I'll remember it.' And two hours later... 'What was that?' When you write it down it can become a key moment for a piece. It's really important to capture that. **Hofesh Shechter**

If I don't have a notepad on me I'm very upset. I like to write a lot, stuff I've read, things I've seen, music I've listened to. **Kenrick Sandy**

Always try to document what you do and watch back and think how you can improve. Really evaluate yourself. Look at it and think, how could I improve that? Have I been dynamic? Do I need a different contrast to my movements? Maybe I need to be softer, stronger, have more precision. Have a look at other people's choreography. Don't copy it, try to take it to the next level. **Marlon Wallen**

Change your methods. Some people have the same way of working and that's it, but I like to think each show has a different ritual, a different method. I'll change lots of different things, like the way the schedule works, or one show I decided not to use a notebook, to feel more spontaneous. That was good. **Arthur Pita**

You are operating in a very slippery world of belief, tiredness and energy. Sometimes the advice is quite basic. Working after lunchtime is just not productive for me, so I do shorter rehearsals after lunch. It's stuff like that. **Hofesh Shechter**

Sometimes you can have too many weeks' rehearsals. You start messing with it just because you've seen it too many times. I'd say four or five weeks is enough. For *Anything Goes* we had something like seven weeks and I was giving people notes on their eyelashes by the end. **Stephen Mear**

Titles, that's an interesting question. So many choreographers use titles that seem like made-up words; I can't tell one from the other. So I think titles for the public, particularly, are very important. It sells more tickets, it literally does. And it gives people a way in. You can surprise them when they get there. **Matthew Bourne**

Understanding composition is important. In the same way you learn composition in music, you can learn compositional things in choreography. If I had to do sonata form in choreography, I could do it. There is something useful about that rigour of understanding – what are some of the structural ways of making dance? **Wayne McGregor**

Most of the time we're all winging it. No one really knows what they're doing. We all have a vision of what we think we're going to create, but usually it never ends up like that. If you do it properly you'll go on a journey and it'll blossom into something completely different, but you have to be ready to let that happen. **Aaron Sillis**

It's like Fellini says about film: you have a dream and it looks fantastic in your head, and then you go to a rehearsal space and it isn't like the dream. It's a real person and a real table. It'll never look like the dream. But you start rehearsing, eventually you get onto the stage, the set, someone throws a bit of light, the make-up, it's getting there. Suddenly someone will drop a sleeve on a costume or something and eventually – ah! – that is the dream. **Arthur Pita**

It's great to build a number then pull it back. When we did *Mary Poppins*, 'Step in Time' is such a long number you can't just keep building and building, you'd self-combust. It's great if you've got a dance arranger to do the music – they sit with you and play the piano and arrange the dance numbers – so you can scrap what's there and make it your own. You can start off slow, build the number, pull it back, do a slow section, do a blues section. It's all about how you layer it. **Stephen Mear**

I would say rule number one is: never remain satisfied. Always keep looking at your work, it can always evolve. **Arthur Pita**

I think the biggest defining factor that will help anyone as a choreographer is that sense of your own vision, your taste, a voice that's not derivative, that there's an honesty about. **Maxine Doyle**

You've got to be true to yourself, otherwise you're trying to predict trends. Don't try and do the thing that seems popular now – everyone wants to be Hofesh Shechter at the moment – be true to yourself and become the next thing. When you're doing something different enough you're Marmite, and that's a good reaction to have early on. The thing they said about me was, 'It's too commercial.' But stick to your guns. If it is something you're passionate about, you can't really do anything else. **Matthew Bourne**

Something I read recently, it was William Forsythe's advice. He said, 'Make what you want to see.' **Arthur Pita**

You have this crazy idea when you're young that you become a choreographer and then you've arrived and it gets easier. But I've noticed I get more and more nervous as I make more and more pieces. The expectation on myself is higher. You realise how much you don't know. You see all your mistakes, but that's what drives you on. You've not solved the problem of choreography. You've not made masterpiece after masterpiece. I don't think it's a problem, but it is a constant quest and constant doubt. It's an art form of doubt. **Wayne McGregor**

Surround yourself with the best people and they'll make your choreography look even better. **Stephen Mear**

What makes good choreography? I think an awareness of craft, style and aesthetic is one thing, but it's the ability to be able to organise a movement language and to be able to say with that what you choose. To be in control of that language so you become the writer of your own work, that's the most important thing. Identify early on what the triggers are for you, whether that is music or something human or theatrical. **Maxine Doyle**

I don't even know what good choreography is. I know there is a sense of satisfaction when something is revealed, or something happens and you think, 'That's really curious,' or you had an image or a vision and it came to life perfectly. That's very satisfying. But I always feel when I start a new piece that I'm back to square one. You start from scratch each time. **Hofesh Shechter**

Never trust an expert, I say. It's dangerous to look to other choreographers' processes for your own making. It's useful as an object to bounce off from, but you don't want to be replicating. You want to find your own way. Make up your own rules. **Wayne McGregor**

Getting Yourself Out There

There's no use making great choreography if no one knows you're doing it. Just as dancers need to get themselves noticed when they're starting out, so do choreographers. What's the best way to get your work out there? And should you follow your creative path single-mindedly, or just take what you can get?

I think having a career in this industry is fifty per cent talent and fifty per cent tenacity. **Maxine Doyle**

No show is too small. The first show I ever put myself out there for was a fashion show in Stratford shopping centre, and once people saw that they said, 'Come and do this show', 'Come and do that show.' **Kenrick Sandy**

Initially, say yes to everything. It's very, very difficult to make a living as a choreographer. There's a handful of people that do and most do more commercial work. Even people that we know, who are well-known names, do not make a good living. When you do your own work, you end up paying for it yourself sometimes. **Matthew Bourne**

For a good decade, I took any job that came my way. **Kate Prince**

I made as much work as I could and I would work very hard at getting people to come and see it, making phone calls, sending letters. I would write my own press releases, setting up meetings with anybody and everybody that I thought might be useful. You have to be really forthright. In some ways when I was younger it was easier, I had a blind confidence. **Maxine Doyle**

Get an agent who understands what you do. They're not going to find you commissions from a dance company, they will find you the other stuff that keeps you going, a little job doing a play somewhere, a helpful sideline. **Matthew Bourne**

Become very articulate about your work, be able to sell it in those face-to-face meetings with promoters and festivals. Document your work as you go along. It's much easier now because of social media. With Facebook and video editing you can do your own self-promotion really beautifully. **Maxine Doyle**

Confidence is one of the major things you need to have, in order to talk, to promote, to create, to innovate. **Kenrick Sandy**

I love to see a hungry choreographer, looking for opportunities. There is no harm in saying, 'This is what I've got to offer, is there any way you can help, or direct me to someone who could.' And that is an ongoing thing. You can't just do it once and then give up. It's a constant drive to find different and exciting ways in which your work can be seen, helped, produced and curated. **Wayne McGregor**

You have to be versatile. My partner Arthur [Pita] has forged a career by saying yes to everything and has become extremely versatile, doing opera, theatre and his own work. Actors call him up and say, 'Can you come and do a session with me, I'm doing a character and want to know how to move.' All these things help form a career. **Matthew Bourne**

What really helps when approaching a company is that you've done your research and that you've seen them. If you've never bothered coming to see us, I'm not sure you'd be the right person to choreograph for us. Just like I wouldn't say, 'You sound super totes famous and I would love it if you would bring some of that fame over to Ballet Black.' **Cassa Pancho**

I meet young choreographers who are very picky. They say, 'I don't want to do that little festival.' But take whatever you can. Yeah, they're not paying you, you'll have to get your own flight and you'll be performing in a lobby, but it's a performance and you're going to learn something, you're going to engage with an audience. Sitting at home and waiting for Sadler's Wells to call, that's not going to happen. **Hofesh Shechter**

I think on every project you can meet interesting people. Keep your eyes open to who you know, who you meet, who's available to you and who's going to make your work more exciting. Be proactive and sensitive at the same time. You don't want to go and push yourself on everybody. **Maxine Doyle**

I remember I made seventy-three VHS cassettes and sent them to all the venues I could think of. Maybe two people wrote back. Now you can send a three-minute clip to 1,000 venues in one click. If I got two responses from seventy-three videos, I might get twenty responses from 1,000. If even one or two happen, then that's something. **Hofesh Shechter**

Everybody has to be entrepreneurial in the way they get their commissions. The question of why there aren't so many women choreographers often comes up. I get sent a lot of videos at the Opera House to look at, and they're very infrequently from females. **Wayne McGregor**

Every week I get minimum of five requests from choreographers and I cannot remember the last time one was from a woman. **Cassa Pancho**

Practicalities:
The Business of Choreography

*Being creative isn't enough to be a successful choreographer.
Whether you're working freelance or setting up your own company, you'll have to deal with the practicalities of budgets and
fees, of finding rehearsal space and finding an audience. What
advice can our choreographers give?*

How do you get rehearsal space with no money?
Sometimes I think the best thing is to open your mouth
and ask. Do voluntary work to get space. If there's a dance
studio, volunteer to do something there in exchange for
some rehearsal space. **Kenrick Sandy**

I started choreographing Hot Gossip in someone's living
room. We had no space I could afford, I didn't have any
money. And that still goes on. People are pulling
together wonderful pieces of work that they're making
in all kinds of spaces just to try and get their work seen.
Arlene Phillips

You have to balance your financial priorities with your
creative priorities. I was a community dance animateur
for two-and-a-half years when I first came to London. I
taught every day, I did tea dances at the weekends. In the
evenings, I made choreography in the school gym.
Wayne McGregor

I think a business mind or a partner who can help you with that is important. That's where we lose people, I think. **Matthew Bourne**

When we were starting out, doing a lot of sponsorship in kind was the way we survived. Getting our programmes printed for free by the local printer but giving them a free advert in return. When we did *Into the Hoods* all our clothing was sponsored by Nike, but they got their clothing on stage in the West End in return. **Kate Prince**

In the beginning, I really enjoyed the business side of it. I thought of it like a chess game: I want people to see this work, I want to be in the place where festivals are inviting me to perform – who do I speak with? I remember not feeling precious about it. I didn't feel like my life depended on it. It was like a game. The strategy was simple: try to get the work seen by as many people as possible. **Hofesh Shechter**

I don't run the business side of our company because I tried for about seven years and I was terrible at it. The truth of it is, making money in dance is incredibly difficult and we're not there yet. We survive but we're not raking it in. **Kate Prince**

You have to understand how budgets work and all those boring things. You have to create within the means you have and that sometimes can be brilliant because it can make you come up with things that are completely original. For *Spitfire* it was just four men in underwear. I could just go to Marks & Spencer and buy the underwear and you could perform it anywhere. You can create little gems. **Matthew Bourne**

It's having a vision and saying, 'Okay, if I want to turn this into a business I need to start learning.' Find out about how other companies developed their business – branding, logos, business cards. Build yourself a showreel, a website, a business plan, then structure your goals for each month or each year. Have a plan of action and keep pushing it out there. Keep knocking on doors. **Marlon Wallen**

Nurturing your audience is really important. Develop a fanbase. We [Punchdrunk] have worked really hard to keep people with us and make them feel they're part of the work. They're your bread and butter. **Maxine Doyle**

If you want to develop your career strategically, you need to be going and meeting people. We're talking about personal one-to-one contact – you can't just do that by email or sending out a video. Put yourself in the situation where you can get your work seen by directors and dancers you want to work with. And you can do all of those things by pushing. I don't think you have to be pushy, but you have to have a strategic mind for the business side. There's no point in just being in the studio all the time and not having that business acumen. **Wayne McGregor**

If you're setting up a company, first of all, what is unique about the company you want to set up? What's going to set you apart to funding people, sponsors, dancers, choreographers, venues? Are you doing a tiny, cheap version of what somebody else bigger is doing? That might be okay, you might be a streamlined, easy-to-tour version of, say, ENB. But does the dance world need that? You have to have a unique product. **Cassa Pancho**

One thing I always try to do is make sure I have a piece to go to after the one I'm making, in case that piece goes terribly wrong. I say that in a flip way but it's really empowering to know that your whole world isn't going to collapse on the basis of what people say about this one piece. When I was younger I would do an education piece, a piece in opera, a little video. Work in lots of different domains, a portfolio approach. **Wayne McGregor**

I threw a lot of money into my career in the first two or three years, in the high thousands, money from my family. It was necessary, otherwise you're just sitting at home. Apply for as much funding as you can, put yourself out there for bursaries. But don't put the cart before the horse. Don't do all your applications when you don't have work. Nobody's going to buy anything that is not there. Do the artistic work first, do it to the best of your ability, and once you have that you can try and do business. **Hofesh Shechter**

7
A Life in Dance

Moving Up the Ranks

Breaking into the industry is one thing, but how do you steer your career after that? How much control can you have over the roles you dance, the companies you work for and the opportunities that come your way? Our dancers talk about making the right choices, dealing with the ups and downs, and how to move up the ranks.

I never said out loud that I was ambitious. I always hoped that my dancing would do the talking. I rose up quite quickly then I plateaued for a long time, and I remember saying to a director, 'Right, well, I'm just going to dance so well that you're not even going to question putting me down for x, y, and z roles.' I wanted her to see that it was a given. And so I just worked harder and harder. **Lauren Cuthbertson**

Work with good teachers and be selective. Don't waste your time. If you see results, stick with them. If you realise this is not what you need, find someone else. Always get good teachers and good mentors, reliable people you can count on to prepare you for particular roles, for everyday class, or to come back from injury. **Tamara Rojo**

Pick people to work with that you want to learn from. There are so many commercial dancers that get stuck in the rut of thinking this is really glamorous, dancing with all these pop stars, that they lose their love for the dance. It can be battered out of you in that pop world, because you're a backing dancer, it's not really about you. **Aaron Sillis**

Constant re-evaluation is what I would recommend. Because your needs and desires change, and if you're not aware of them you can end up fighting for things, running after things, and being sucked into a life you didn't want for yourself. **Seeta Patel**

One thing I learned very early on: don't get stuck in your childhood dreams. You have an idea of what or where you want to dance, and sometimes that doesn't happen. The interesting thing is that other doors will open and your career will be a lot more fascinating than you imagined. So don't be stubborn, allow the room to discover new patterns and new directions. **Tamara Rojo**

You need to be prepared to change course. If you're working with a director who doesn't appreciate what you have to offer, find an environment better suited to developing your skills and talent. You might have to move country. Of course, not a lot of people will be willing to do that. You might have to go to Spain or France, learn another language. I did that – it's not easy – but for me it was survival. **Carlos Acosta**

It's important to keep challenging yourself, but I think that can sometimes be misinterpreted as constantly doing something new or grossly different rather than an internal refinement. **Seeta Patel**

Sometimes I feel dancers can be the most uncreative people, because they become so concentrated on doing something in the way they've been told, to please other people, that they forget to breathe and to grow. **Lauren Cuthbertson**

Some people like to compete with others in order to get better. I never needed that. For me it's just about becoming better than I was the day before, that's what motivates me. We're either ripening or rotting; we either go one way or the other. We're never completely at a standstill. So as long as you're still ripening, you're progressing the right way. **Tommy Franzén**

At Houston Ballet I had an amazing life, a very nice house, I was doing all the opening nights. And then I said to myself, 'Is this the life I wanted to live?' Because being a great dancer in Houston doesn't mean you're a great dancer in the bigger leagues. I really wanted to see how big I could be. A lot of people said I was crazy when I came to London. **Carlos Acosta**

It's really easy to get tunnel vision. You think, 'I'm injured, I haven't got a job, everything's terrible.' But people who make their own opportunities control their careers much more. **Cassa Pancho**

Some people say, 'Oh, I was never given the role.' Wrong, it is you that's to blame. Your determination is yours. Somebody can say they're not going to cast you, but your love of dancing is yours. Nobody owns that. **Carlos Acosta**

I find pigeonholing is something that happens to me quite often. I'd always end up being cast in very similar roles. But that's not about my ability, that's a lack of vision of the choreographer. **Seeta Patel**

I always believed that my work would speak for itself. And when that's not the case, try to have a constructive dialogue with your director. Sometimes things are perceived a certain way because we don't see the whole picture. It's better to talk about it than to guess, because usually guess-ing gets you on to really unsteady ground. **Tamara Rojo**

Sometimes you have to be willing to wait. But when I see there is another dancer doing roles that I could do better than them, I will confront that. You have to push and say, 'This is what I want,' and then fight for it. With-out stepping on anybody, without being mean to anybody. Every day you come in and do your stretches, watch your videos, rehearse on your own. Then when these opportunities come, you're going to be ready. You'll fly. **Carlos Acosta**

Rivalries and Relationships

Dance is a hugely competitive industry, and if certain portrayals of the dance world were to be believed, it's a hotbed of sadistic directors and jealous rivalries between dancers. Is it really like that? The dancers give some advice on keeping good professional relationships and not succumbing to the green-eyed monster.

I loved company life. I loved the camaraderie of a big company. Of course it can be tough, there's competition, people fighting for roles, people get upset – not quite like *Black Swan*. But dancing with other people is a huge pleasure. **Arthur Pita**

When I first joined the company, everybody thought I was a total bitch. I came across as cold, but it's because my desire in the studio was to work, not to socialise. And I was terrified. But in recent years I've been able to sit and have a conversation with someone rather than being competitive and thinking, 'I have to be better than you.' When you look at other dancers, you should never be envious of what they are. **Melissa Hamilton**

Jealousy? It goes with the territory. Everybody's striving and they all want something, and if they feel you don't deserve it there will be a lot of jealousy and a lot of behind-your-back talk, which you can hear. You have to be able to switch off and focus on what is important for you. And be genuine and honest. As soon as people get to know you they often won't be as critical. **Darcey Bussell**

I think there's always an element of insecurity. There are so many dancers around. I work with a lot of good dancers that can do things I can't do, and vice versa. I would say, remember you got the job for a reason. Just learn from them and share. That's the most important thing. Don't be protective over your moves, either. **Tommy Franzén**

The commercial scene can be very pretentious, it can be very business-minded. It's not about friendship. You have to have tolerance against any negative energy. The only person that can stop you from doing what you're doing is yourself. They may not give you a job, but it doesn't mean you shouldn't be working. **Kenrick Sandy**

I think jealousy is less common than people think. Most dancers are too concerned with themselves. Everyone used to talk about me and Alina [Cojocaru, being rivals]. The truth is we're both such perfectionists, that rarely do we look around. I've never, ever looked at a casting and added up how many shows other people have. I know some people do that but it's pointless. If you're happy with what you're given, do it. If you're unhappy, talk about it. Just don't compare yourself to someone else. **Tamara Rojo**

Don't waste your time being jealous. Because the chances are someone else is looking at you in exactly the same way. It's almost infectious, that behaviour. I feel like I've been much freer in my career by not being jealous and by being inspired instead. **Lauren Cuthbertson**

I've never been one of those people that are jealous. Well, I have, but I don't show it. **Matthew Rees**

I have such a high standard of people I work with, I treat them with the utmost respect and I expect that back. I treat them as friends, but I know where to draw the line. I hear about choreographers that yell and scream... but I'm no pushover. When I want quiet in a room, I have quiet in a room. And in return I hopefully give my dancers some of the best jobs they'll do. **Stephen Mear**

I work with one director who has the most amazing way of getting what he wants. He listens to everybody, he absolutely loves whatever it is that they have brought, 'Absolutely! That's just what I want.' Then he'll go, 'You know... we could think about this...' and then he throws in an idea, 'That's what you were thinking, wasn't it?' And he gets his own way. It's just beautiful the way he does it. It's a real art. **Arlene Phillips**

Keeping the Faith

A dancer's life can be exhausting, not just physically. Our dancers give some advice on coping with the roller coaster, from riding out the lean times, to managing the intensity of performance, and staying creatively inspired along the way.

The lifestyle of a dancer can be very difficult sometimes. There's a lot of partying that goes along with it. Performing at night, it can be 10.30 or 11 when you leave the theatre and you can't come down quickly. Some people go out for those couple of hours and then you're never getting the downtime, you're straight in to the next day. When I did Twyla Tharp's *Movin' Out*, I didn't touch alcohol until the closing-night party. I'd come off stage feeling completely exhausted and drained, go home to sleep, wake up feeling like I couldn't get through the show again. I'd warm up, do company class, have one-hundred-and-ten per cent energy for the show and then come off stage and feel like I was going to die. A lot of the time it's like that. **Aaron Sillis**

Dancers are so underestimated because their discipline is stronger than anyone's. Stronger than any actor. **Stephen Mear**

I always think that dancers are the blue-collar workers of theatre. We work much harder than anyone else. In musical theatre you're doing all that stuff to keep the show going, you're the first ones in, the last ones out. In so many operas I've done, if the dancers had a revolution, the whole thing would fall apart. Yet they're paid terribly. But it never breaks the spirit. I think dancers are tough. **Arthur Pita**

We had a sixty-date tour, and then it went from sixty to a hundred and fourteen dates. We were shattered. We thought we were going to have to get some replicants of Flawless to do the remaining dates. That's really, really intense. You're knackered and you just want a holiday, but we learned each other's roles, so if someone felt too tired that day, we were able to swap things over. **Marlon Wallen**

In musical theatre you know you've signed for a year. Don't start slacking halfway through. You'll get a bad reputation and that will get out before your next audition. **Stephen Mear**

We did a performance in High Wycombe or somewhere. There were two people in the audience: one man in the front row and another person in the middle asleep. I thought, we've been making this piece for six weeks, dying, slogging, researching. That was heartbreaking. But you deliver. I remember we looked at each other, 'Okay, we're just doing this for each other.' **Arthur Pita**

The worst thing is that the artistic process is painful, and it's consuming – that's maybe the best thing as well. It's hard when you have a family and you're doing a project. My partner says I disappear. I might be present in the room with them, but I'm not with them. **Maxine Doyle**

I don't think there's any excuse for stasis. For example, if I've not got anything on for the next couple of months, I would go volunteering. I would go volunteering in Ethiopia and do an education programme while I'm there. Or I would hit all the London galleries, spend time getting to know the artists better and do a hit list of potential subjects for pieces I'd be interested in making. You can always be creatively engaged. **Wayne McGregor**

It is exhausting running a company and it can be very difficult to keep going with these things, but I remind myself that it was no one else's idea and if I don't like it, tough. I've taken them this far, I can't ditch them now. **Cassa Pancho**

The toughest thing for me is self-discipline. Unless you're working for a company where someone's paying you to be there, you have to get up and do a bunch of stuff even though you're not being paid for it. When I get disheartened, I look at the alternative, of working a desk job, the temping I've done, and I'm reminded I'm not ready to be there. There's nothing else I want to do more. I'm not done with dance yet. **Seeta Patel**

How do you keep the faith? See something inspiring – for me it could be a movie – keep working, go to classes. I just had the faith. It's about passion, ultimately, working in this industry. If you don't have that passion that drives you, if you're not occupied and consumed by the process of wanting to make something every day, you might as well go and work in the City and earn loads of money. **Maxine Doyle**

After a while you have to ask yourself some questions. Not everyone's good, simple as that. I know today it's all about, 'If you dream it, you can have it,' but you're not owed a living. Just because you've decided to call yourself a choreographer or a dancer, doesn't mean you're going to have a career as one. That's a hard acceptance to come to terms with. **Matthew Bourne**

Making Ends Meet

There are many, many wonderful things about being a dancer, but unless you're a star ballerina or a TV celebrity, making a lot of money probably isn't one of them. Equity minimum rates start at £320 per week, and with many dancers working freelance, it's often necessary to juggle jobs in order to balance creative fulfilment and paying the rent. Recent figures from Dancers Pro show that only nine per cent of dancers surveyed didn't have to take on non-dancing work. So should you be looking for another job? Is it ever okay to work for nothing? And, importantly, can you ask for a raise?

Financially, it's really difficult if you're a freelancer. Rates haven't gone up; I'm paid the same as when I left college. But I look at other professions and think I shouldn't feel too sorry for myself because I'm doing something I really love. **Jonathan Goddard**

In a ballet company, you know what you're getting paid. In hip-hop companies normally you're employed for a project, for a few months. In the commercial world you've got more earning potential, but it's a lot of short gigs and dry spells, a lot of insecurity – which I actually like. I like to leave it open and be flexible. For some people that's the worst thing they could imagine. It's difficult to have both freedom and security, and freedom is more important to me. **Tommy Franzén**

As a dancer, you need another job. There's just no question about it. My own daughter was in musical theatre and I said to her, you need to have something else you can do. To her credit, my daughter studied make-up and now she is actually a very successful make-up artist. When that moment came and she thought, 'I don't want to dance any more,' she was ready to take on a job and make that her career. **Arlene Phillips**

Most people will have to take some other job at some point and there's nothing wrong with that. I've always quite fancied working in London Zoo or in a garden centre if I was out of work. You have to earn a living. **Adam Garcia**

I know some really talented dancers who spend half their year doing promo work, standing in Waterloo Station trying to sell a new conditioner, because work comes when it comes. I know a great dancer who started her own dog-sitting company and she does that when she's not performing. I think they're smart. We're all freelance and you've got to have something to pay your way. **Kate Prince**

Dance is so competitive, it would be crazy not to think of doing something else, and most logically, people turn to teaching. Then again, the greats like Tamara Rojo or Marianela Nuñez, maybe those people don't think like that and that's how they're so single-minded in their drive. It's like people who mortgage their home to finance their movie. I would never do that. But maybe those rare people who would, that's why they are where they are. **Cassa Pancho**

Be open to everything. I do movement direction, I do marketing as well. I do some musicals. I've taught all the way through my career. I try to keep them all going and I like seeing all the different working environments. I find it really useful to get an overview of everything. **Jonathan Goddard**

I took some of the worst jobs you could imagine because I needed money to live. One of the worst jobs I ever did was in Dagenham, folding old army greatcoats that were coming out of boxes in mothballs from wars all around the world to be sold in Kensington Market. For a year I did that job, starting at seven in the morning, and at the end of the day I'd go to class smelling like a mothball. **Arlene Phillips**

I've been in the position of training every day and having to juggle education and dance and part-time work. It's all possible, it's just a matter of time-management. **Marlon Wallen**

I've always earned money, because I couldn't pay for my props or rent a studio without it. I worked in a bar, I worked as a PA, but in my first week I thought, 'I can't do this any more.' I used to spend all my time on the phone setting up projects for when I would leave in six months' time. It made me more resolute actually. **Maxine Doyle**

It's okay for a choreographer to work for nothing, but not for a dancer. I always really tried to pay the dancers, even if it wasn't a lot. Don't expect people to make a sacrifice for you. **Hofesh Shechter**

Asking for more money is difficult, because a lot of the time you're working for people you know. The producer is the person to get to. I think understanding what's going on helps. If it was more popular you'd be paid more. You can't ask for more money if there are only twenty people coming to watch. **Jonathan Goddard**

You do get paid well when you play leads in musicals. The producers are certainly getting paid well and I want some of that. **Adam Garcia**

The advice about getting paid is really difficult. When I first started getting work, I was accepting really low fees, which was fine from my point of view, I just wanted to do the job – 'He says he's only got a hundred quid.' But it shoots the industry in the foot because they always know they can find someone to do it cheaper and that's the real problem. **Kate Prince**

I'm not a good negotiator. That's why I have a very good agent. Do the maths: count up the seats, the average ticket price, see how full it is. See what the producers are making per week and see if you deserve any more of that. Negotiate for more. The threat, as we all know, is that there's someone else who can do your job. But I guess your job in the audition is to impress them enough that they say, 'We really want to work with this person.' **Adam Garcia**

I would say to everyone, don't dance in a music video for nothing. They can afford it, or you shouldn't be there. **Kate Prince**

Dance is not money-spinning. That's why I went into the movies. **Adam Garcia**

Dealing with Criticism

Most dancers are perfectionists and no stranger to self-criticism, but that doesn't mean it doesn't sting when judgement comes from outside. Dance training can feel like a constant stream of criticism, then you get into the professional world and the corrections don't stop. How do you stay sane? Here's what the dancers have to say...

You can't please everybody. You can't even please yourself half the time. **Lauren Cuthbertson**

In this industry, people are constantly going to put you down, because everybody is trying to get somewhere. It doesn't have to be that way, but it is. **Melissa Hamilton**

If you don't get criticism you should worry, because that means they don't care. If they actually have something to say then they believe you can improve. I have a lot of kids saying, 'I've had too much criticism, I don't even want to attempt it now.' It's about seeing that criticism as a positive, not a negative, and that's up to you. **Darcey Bussell**

Criticism is good if you can use it to your advantage. I remember somebody telling me once that I danced with my mouth open all the time. The next performance after that I was actively aware of my mouth being open. But I think it can be detrimental if you start focusing on that too much. **Aaron Sillis**

You get corrections all the time. You should just take them on and try to understand them in a calm way. There's a human instinct to protest: 'But I was trying to…' But with dance you're best to sit with the correction for a bit, try and work out what that person's seeing and where that's coming from. **Jonathan Goddard**

Take the notes, take them on board, smile, say yes, do it. I'm a big believer in never giving general notes. If I know somebody's doing it wrong, I always do a name-and-shame. This isn't being horrible, this is to make you not look stupid. **Stephen Mear**

In Vaganova training, they're very critical. To the point where you feel you can't move. I changed to RAD and it changed my mind about how I critiqued myself. You're not perfect; perfection is kind of boring sometimes. I like to see a little bit of risk and a little bit of 'go for it'. You can't be highly self-critical if you're going to try and show something new. **Matthew Golding**

The majority of the time, I take criticism with a pinch of salt. I know I'm presenting work that is complicated and takes time to understand, and I'm not willing to compromise on that. It isn't going to be for everyone. **Seeta Patel**

I have had experiences with people who can be quite malicious or psychological, and that is hard. Some choreographers will keep trying to pull it back to something personal about you, as an effort to break the psyche, and you just have to see that for what it is. **Jonathan Goddard**

Not everyone's going to give you good advice. You need to learn how to filter that. Learn to trust certain people. If you have certain friends around you that you know will give you a genuine reaction and opinion, I think that is incredibly valuable. **Steven McRae**

I'm not very good at dealing with criticism, to be honest. It could just be one person's opinion, but it's worth having a think about what triggered that person to say that. Maybe you can learn from it. I would make sure that next time there is no opportunity to give me a bad comment. **Tommy Franzén**

One thing people have to learn is not to be blind. Know your range. Your range might be dictated by your body. And someone might, at some point, acknowledge that. If you don't have the facilities to lead a ballet, try to do your best, for you. Every Romeo needs a Mercutio. **Carlos Acosta**

I try not to let any success or failure get to my head too much. I'm an extremely sensitive person and I get blocked easily by things that people say. It's hard when you're climbing slowly through whatever hierarchy there is, and it's scary when you're in it by yourself. It's hard to maintain perspective and sanity through all of that. I guess that's where the challenge is. **Seeta Patel**

I think the best way to critique something is see yourself on camera. Then you know that's how you looked. It's tough, but it's the easiest way to find out how you look. **Matthew Golding**

I am my worst critic. I'm always doubting and questioning. Once I've done something, I look at how I'm going to better it. I listen to people close to me, but I'm stubborn in my ways. I want to express myself how I want to express myself, and if I listen to too many people and take all their advice then my piece is no longer mine. **Kenrick Sandy**

With dance, you look to the choreographer or the audience to tell you whether it's good or bad. Somehow the thing exists between you and them. Whereas with actors, that thing exists more *inside* of you. When you get notes about acting, you can feel like you've embarrassed yourself, it's quite personal somehow. Dance can be a bit more neutral; it's good practice to try to be more objective. **Jonathan Goddard**

Self-criticism can block you. You can't be highly critical because then you're not going to go anywhere. **Matthew Golding**

People will tell you at some point that you're not good enough and that you're not going to make it. You only conquer that through success. The more you work, the better technique you develop and the more people notice. The more successful you become, the more confident you will become. It's never the other way round. You're not naturally confident. You become confident because you achieve, and it's a self-fulfilling prophecy. **Tamara Rojo**

In some pop videos I've really felt that the director's hated me and I've been moved to the back or out of the shot. It's really soul-destroying, but if you've got the wrong look or the dance style's not working for them, you can't really change that. What you have to remember is the director and the choreographer are under so many other external pressures, you might be reading too much into something. **Aaron Sillis**

Don't be afraid to take a look at yourself in the mirror. Don't always think you're right. **Stephen Mear**

You have to be clever enough to see where you are, to see your possibilities and to see, when someone tells you you're not going to make it, whether they could be right to a certain extent, or if they're doing it as an act of meanness and frustration. There are a lot of people frustrated in this career. It's not a secret. **Carlos Acosta**

I've been involved in some major flops, but when you're just in there as a choreographer on a bigger production you can walk away relatively unscathed. I did one last year that did terribly badly – the *X Factor* musical – but I managed to get away with it. I hope I did a good job for them, but the show didn't go well. But I still learned a lot doing that. **Kate Prince**

People have different opinions and different ways of teaching, and the truth is there is not just one way to dance. Maybe you are a Balanchine dancer, maybe you are a contemporary dancer, maybe you're a Forsythe dancer, maybe you're a Mats Ek dancer, maybe you are a classical dancer. Don't despair because one particular person doesn't think you fit their opinion of what a dancer is. Open your horizons, go somewhere else, keep studying, keep working and you will get there. **Tamara Rojo**

Asking for Feedback

Mentors, dramaturgs, friends, colleagues; who can you turn to for an honest opinion? And how upfront should you be about asking for feedback?

It's best to have friends who are honest. I did a show called *Tonight's the Night*, with Rod Stewart songs. I remember after the first show, my best friend grabbed my leg and said: 'What were you thinking?!' **Stephen Mear**

In America, generally they come up to you after an audition and they're very upfront. They want to know why they didn't get it so they can damn well go away and work on whatever it was that they've failed on. **Arlene Phillips**

You can ask for feedback. It's good to ask an associate or a dance captain, 'Is there anything I could do to make this better?' It's good to know what it is specifically. You can get a couple of words said to you that will completely change your performance. **Aaron Sillis**

Bring someone in whose opinions you trust. And rather than say, 'Did you like it?' Say, 'What did you see? Tell me what you saw and what did you get from it.' People are always seeing things I didn't expect them to see, or laughing at things I didn't think were funny. There are all sorts of reactions, they shouldn't be wrong or right. **Matthew Bourne**

Ask for advice. Asking for mentorship is a fantastic thing and generally most people are fairly amenable. Even sending a video clip and saying, 'Could you give me a line of feedback?' Ask for something very small that's manageable and that's a connection made. **Jonathan Goddard**

Seek mentors, but do it wisely. There are people with their own agendas. **Seeta Patel**

I personally think there's an over-professionalisation of mentoring, to an extent where there are more mentors getting paid than artists, and all the time you're listening to other people's point of view. The whole point of being an artist is it's your point of view. You have to have time to develop it, which includes making lots of mistakes. I think one has to use mentors judiciously. **Wayne McGregor**

The thing I don't agree with these days is the whole dramaturg thing. If you're going to make a piece, I don't understand why you'd bring someone else in to structure it. That's your job. **Matthew Bourne**

Just because you want to be a choreographer, it doesn't mean you should be. Find someone who can look at your work and say, 'Hey, you're a genius,' or, 'Halfway through it starts to drag.' I think there's a lot of self-indulgence in the dance world. It's not deliberate, but it takes a lot of discipline to look at your work and see what it needs. You need someone to tell you. You need an editor. **Cassa Pancho**

Reviews: Do You Read Them?

Can you bear to look? Do you sneak a glance at the star ratings? Do you trawl Twitter in the small hours looking for any mention of your name? Is reading reviews a recipe for self-destruction or a constructive way to improve your performance? Our dancers don't always agree on this one...

Criticism never gets easier. I remember when I did The Place Prize there was a big article with a big picture, but it was not a happy review. I was so deflated. 'But I did my best!' I remember John Ashford, the director at The Place, telling me, 'You're going to have to learn to live with that.' **Hofesh Shechter**

I read all reviews. I love dance writing. It fires something in my brain. You start to imagine the performance in your head and even that is choreographic – it's exercising that part of your brain that's about visualisation of movement. You get an overview of what's going on, you can sound informed, and hopefully you might go and see some of this stuff. It's your world, it's your job to learn about it. **Jonathan Goddard**

The best criticism can play a fantastic part in the overall development of an art form. At its worst I think it's snippy and not that useful and it's best to park it. But it's useful to have people say, 'This is what I received from the thing that you made.' Whether you intended that or not, that's their reality of it. **Wayne McGregor**

I read all the reviews. I used to take them terribly personally, a long time ago, but choreography is so subjective. If you came and hated one piece and loved another, well, that's just your taste. It's out there for a couple of days and then everyone's forgotten about it. **Cassa Pancho**

You can't take anything good to heart unless you're going to take the bad stuff to heart as well. You've either got to be okay with the positive and negative, or just don't read any of it. **Kate Prince**

People criticising your work, it's temporary. It's only a snapshot of that one piece. It's not of your whole choreographic career, it's just what they're thinking at that moment. **Wayne McGregor**

Criticism can sometimes almost energise you. It can make you think: either I believe in this piece or I don't. If I don't believe in the piece then that's harder, but then I have to deal with that anyway. **Hofesh Shechter**

Personally I read everything, because I like to know the whole picture. You start to understand the filters and preferences of certain critics, their snapshot of the world. I've always found that, even in the most brutal criticisms, there's always either a kernel of truth or a question that's useful to you. **Wayne McGregor**

I don't read them all. I don't go on Twitter because I hate it. I think the internet is mean. **Kate Prince**

I don't read Facebook, I don't go on Twitter, I don't read newspaper reviews, I stay away from all that stuff. It's not going to change me that much. Some people really want good reviews and that's important to them, but it's never been important to me. **Matthew Golding**

I've stopped reading reviews for the last five years. I remember doing *On the Town* and got the worst reviews from the ballet critics. Two years later we did it again and I changed eight counts in the show, but in the meantime I'd won an Olivier Award and then these same critics suddenly said I was the best thing ever, had pulled everything out of the bag. 'He's at the top of his career!' And I said, that's it, ignorance is bliss. **Stephen Mear**

Dance performance is very momentary. You can have a good night and a bad night. People see the work and say it changed completely from two days ago, and it's the same work. But it can look different, with the energy and the audience. Concentrate on the art and take the rest quite lightly. **Hofesh Shechter**

I feel that British people are always a bit sceptical of their own. When you've finished your career you might be commended, you might have left a nice stamp, but while it's going on it doesn't feel like that. **Lauren Cuthbertson**

We've never had a problem with getting audiences and that can be very empowering. So you can balance the criticism and the critique around the work with the fact that also people often really enjoy it. They will pay money to come and watch it in their thousands. **Wayne McGregor**

I can sometimes find great things in criticism and it will make me want to work my performance differently, but it's just someone's opinion. If they're critical about one aspect of your performance that the director doesn't have an issue with, then you don't want to be starting to change your performance based on a viewer's critique. **Aaron Sillis**

At the end of the day, are you happy with what you did, yourself? You know the mistakes you made. **Kate Prince**

Do I take in the reviews? Not really. Sometimes I don't even read them. I did not put myself in this field for these people. All they're going to do is look at my work, criticise it, then move on to the next piece. Whereas I will continue creating work. I'm not energised by critics, I'm energised by the passion and love for what I do. I have a very 'don't care' attitude. I like to be raw, I like to be real, I like to be honest. **Kenrick Sandy**

It's an audience of one, I'm afraid. That's not being arrogant, and not saying you're not thinking about the audience, but yourself is the only audience you can have. **Wayne McGregor**

It can be difficult because you're very exposed. You have social media where everybody says what they want. I feel like this statue in a public square and people can come and throw something at me, pour beer on me, and I can't really respond. But it's not really me. I made the work, but it's not me. Making the work and then the separation of coming back to my simple little life is really good. **Hofesh Shechter**

At the end of the day, it's only dancing. And I'm obsessed and passionate and it is my whole life, but it *is* only dancing. **Wayne McGregor**

Life After Dance

It used to be said that a dancer's career ended at thirty-five, but plenty of dancers these days are overturning those expectations. Sylvie Guillem retired aged fifty, and Merce Cunningham was still performing in his seventies. But compared with other professions, dancers' careers are undeniably short, even for those who remain unscathed by injury. When you've trained so hard to do something you're so passionate about, how do you cope with saying goodbye to a dancer's life? And where do you go next?

Retiring is always tough because dancing is the only thing you know about yourself. That is your strength. When you suddenly don't have that, you feel lost. Suddenly you're on your own. I made sure I had other distractions as soon as I retired, other things to focus on. That's what helped me cope. And there are so many ways of using all the disciplines you have from dance in your everyday life. **Darcey Bussell**

I like to plan. I'm a bit of a control freak and, when I tore my Achilles, it freaked me out how fragile this career is. I finished a degree in Business Management and Leadership last Christmas, spread out over five years with the Open University. I look at it as a positive rather than a negative that the career is short. We're forced into another career. **Steven McRae**

Injury can finish a career in moments and it is absolutely tragic. I often feel that dancers are never prepared for that, and that's why I worry when dancers want to leave school and not take any exams. You need to keep your mind going. You need to keep something there for that moment when you're not dancing any more. **Arlene Phillips**

I do think it's important to think about the wider picture, even while you're dancing. I'm always impressed with the guys in my company, Random. I've got one dancer who learnt Spanish, one who studied an MA in Philosophy at the same time as performing, one doing Medieval History. It helps with perspective. That's partly why I like to work outside the realm of dance, with scientists, because I think there is another world and we often get so focused on our little bubble. **Wayne McGregor**

I always knew I had to have a plan, a financial plan, for later. Dancers have such a short career and [for freelance dancers] there's no pension; if we're injured we can't earn money. So it's important for a dancer to have some sort of plan B. I trained to be a sports-massage therapist. I see a lot of people going into fitness. Being a personal trainer is a trend at the moment. **Tommy Franzén**

If someone has trained from such a young age to pursue their dream, I think that looks good on anyone's CV. Any employer or education institution that sees the dedication that someone has put in will think it's a bonus. **Steven McRae**

While you're dancing and when you are in your prime, you shouldn't think about retirement. The only thing that you have to have clear is your goal and your dreams and just work for them. That's all it is. What can I learn today and tomorrow? **Carlos Acosta**

It feels like, with contemporary dance, there is a shift in how long a career can be. I like to think that when some things start to drop, other things start to become more mature and taste better. There's a Bharata Natyam dancer in India who started getting more work after the age of seventy. You're not trying to attempt the same things you were doing before – accept that with dignity. **Seeta Patel**

I don't think there's an age to start and I don't think there's an age to end. I've been very inspired by some people who are sixty-plus and still dancing. **Kenrick Sandy**

I remember that very clear moment of bowing on stage at my last show. I looked out and had this satisfaction and thought, 'Tick. You've done that.' I remember looking at everyone on stage and they looked different to me. I saw them carrying on as performers and I felt myself pulling away. But it was a lovely, satisfied feeling. It was like a full meal. I think that's the difference: the hunger goes. **Arthur Pita**

I don't call what I'm going to do retirement, it's transition. I always say an artist never retires, it's only evolution. There are other ways to express your artistry, through books, through choreography. **Carlos Acosta**

I'm seventy-one. I'm forever going to see dance. I went to see *Here Lies Love* last week and I was dancing in the aisles. You can make dance your life as long as you have the passion for it and that passion doesn't die so easily. **Arlene Phillips**

One Piece of Advice

There's one final question I posed to all of our dancers and cho-reographers: If you could just give one piece of advice to an aspiring dancer, what would it be? What did they wish they'd known? What advice would they give their younger selves? Here's what they said…

One piece of advice to someone who wanted to be a dancer? Become an accountant. **Cassa Pancho**

The crucial thing is to dream big and work hard. Because you are only as big as your dreams and how hard you work to make them a reality. If you set your expectations very low, that's all you're going to be. The minute you say, 'I'm satisfied,' you stop growing. **Carlos Acosta**

Spend some time in the studio. Put some music on and just dance around. Feel how you actually want to move. I think all along the way you're buffeted by techniques, but that you need to find freedom at the very beginning and hold on to what it is inside you that wants to move. Otherwise it's so easy to get lost in the pursuit of technique and perfection and the idea of dance that other people impose, rather than what it is for you. **Jonathan Goddard**

The only thing I regret is not having thrown myself in the deep end at a younger age. **Kate Prince**

If you want to be a dancer, learn dance history. Know what you're getting into and learn about the companies that are currently working. My knowledge pre-sixteen was pop-cultural references: Madonna, Michael Jackson, *Grease*, *Dirty Dancing*. I had no other artistic knowledge outside of the commercial genre. I think if I'd had a bit more knowledge beforehand I might have had a clearer vision of where I could go. **Aaron Sillis**

Research everything. Research schools, teachers, companies, repertoire. Find out who's doing what and where, go there as much as you can, take class with everyone. Look at good dancers, research where they studied and go and study there. Look at good companies that you like, try to go and take class with them. **Tamara Rojo**

The first thing I always go by is the Flawless motto: 'Chase the dream, not the competition.' You have the dreams that you want to achieve and don't let anyone get in the way. **Marlon Wallen**

Enjoy it. Do it for enjoyment. Dance in the way that it comes out of you, as much as thinking about anyone else. That's the best way. **Matthew Golding**

Stay focused and don't waste time. In this profession, time is crucial. We're all in a race against time. One year could be the making of a career, or in one year you can be out of a job. **Carlos Acosta**

Watch as much as possible, educate yourself and learn what it is you like. People will give you their opinions throughout your career and you have to have your own, otherwise you'll crumble. Figure out what it is that makes you special and unique – because each and every dancer in every company is. But you need to learn that yourself, because no one's going to spend their time learning it for you. They're all too busy trying to find it themselves. **Melissa Hamilton**

I wish I'd known that, just because other people talk like they know what they're doing, it doesn't mean they know anything. It's okay to stick to your opinion. A lot of times I've been worried about offending somebody. I was usually the youngest person in the room and I'd think, 'Well, if he thinks that and he's forty he must really know.' Now I look back and I can't believe the absolute rubbish that some people talk. **Cassa Pancho**

Listen to advice, but follow your gut. It's such a subjective art form, you can't just listen to someone else's opinion. You have to find the strength to follow your own gut. **Lauren Cuthbertson**

There is so much distraction nowadays in the world and it's very hard to concentrate on one thing. You need to know that you can't have everything. Being a dancer is a lifestyle. It's not just something that occasionally you do. Dance at this level is not for everybody. You have to watch what you eat, you need to go to bed early, you need to put all the energy in one direction and work, work, work. It's how strong you are to really fight for what you want. **Carlos Acosta**

Never, ever give up. It doesn't matter what happens – and there are huge disappointments – I think the best advice is give yourself a day and then move along. Don't give up. **Arlene Phillips**

Glossary

People, productions and terms featured in this book.

Adagio   The section of a ballet class where the dancer executes slow, controlled movements.

Alpha   A step from the funk-dance-style locking (one of the three core hip-hop styles). The dancer falls back on their hands and kicks one or both legs up in the air.

George Balanchine   Russian choreographer (1904–1983) who began his career with the Ballets Russes and went on to define American ballet in the twentieth century. He is thought to have created over four hundred works for stage and screen.

Ballon   In ballet, the light quality of a dancer's jump and their ability seemingly to float suspended in the air.

Barre   The wooden beam on which a dancer rests their hand while they perform exercises. The term also refers to the first section of every ballet class, where these exercises are performed.

Mikhail Baryshnikov   Russian dancer (*b.* 1948) who was one of the exceptional talents of his generation. Baryshnikov began his career with the Kirov Ballet before defecting to Canada in 1974, going on to dance with American Ballet Theatre and New York City Ballet. He continues to perform.

Battling   An important part of hip-hop dance culture, where dancers or crews compete against each other in a game of one-upmanship.

Pina Bausch   German choreographer (1940–2009) who pioneered the art of *tanztheater* (dance theatre) in highly original works, examining the human condition and the absurdities of life through a mix of movement, music, speech and spectacle.

Bharata Natyam   Southern Indian classical dance form, thought to have originated in the Hindu temples of Tamil Nadu some three thousand years ago.

Bolshoi Ballet   One of the two titans of Russian ballet (see also Mariinsky Ballet, below), the ballet company based at the Bolshoi Theatre in Moscow was founded in 1776. *Bolshoi* in Russian means 'big' and the company created its reputation on the dynamism and power of its dancers.

The Brit School   Performing-arts college in Croydon.

Cecchetti   A method of dance teaching named after the Italian ballet master Enrico Cecchetti (1850–1928).

Robert (Bob) Cohan   American dancer and choreographer (*b.* 1925) who performed with the Martha Graham Dance Company and brought contemporary dance to the UK as founder of the London Contemporary Dance School in 1967.

Alina Cojocaru   Romanian ballerina (*b.* 1981) known for her light-as-air quality who danced with the Royal Ballet from 1999–2013, and is currently a lead principal dancer with English National Ballet.

Corps de ballet   The 'chorus' of a ballet company. Those who are not in the leading roles and often perform in unison as an ensemble.

Merce Cunningham   American dancer and choreographer (1919–2009). A hugely influential figure in twentieth-century dance, he pioneered the use of 'chance' methods in composition and developed a distinctive technique which still forms the basis of much contemporary dance training today.

Mats Ek   Swedish dancer and choreographer (*b.* 1945) and former Artistic Director of the Cullberg Ballet.

Elmhurst School for Dance   Full-time ballet school founded in 1922 and now based in Birmingham, linked to Birmingham Royal Ballet.

English National Ballet (ENB)   British touring ballet company, based in London, founded in 1950.

The Five & the Prophecy of Prana   A manga-inspired hip-hip show by Boy Blue Entertainment, created in 2013.

Floor barre   The basic ballet exercises normally performed at the barre, but instead executed sitting or lying on the floor.

William Forsythe   American dancer and choreographer (*b.* 1949) who brought radical changes to classical ballet as director of Ballet Frankfurt in the 1980s.

Fouetté   A ballet step based on a pirouette (see below), where the non-supporting leg is outstretched at ninety degrees and whips around in a circle as the body turns. In *Swan Lake*, the black swan Odile famously performs thirty-two fouetté turns in a row.

Martha Graham   American dancer and choreographer (1894–1991) who was one of the founders of modern dance. The technique she developed, based on principles of contraction and release, remains one of the cornerstones of contemporary dance training today.

Sylvie Guillem French dancer (*b.* 1965) of extraordinary technical ability who was one of the biggest ballet stars of the late-twentieth/early-twenty-first century. Guillem was the youngest *étoile* (top-ranking dancer) at the Paris Opera Ballet aged nineteen, then a principal guest artist with the Royal Ballet from 1989–2007. She retired in 2015, aged fifty.

Here Lies Love Musical by David Byrne and Fatboy Slim about Imelda Marcos, First Lady of the Phillippines, premiered in New York City and transferred to London's National Theatre.

Hot Gossip Dance troupe formed by Arlene Phillips, which performed on television between 1974 and 1986.

Into the Hoods Premiered in 2006, this hip-hop take on classic fairytales by Kate Prince and ZooNation became the longest-running dance show in the West End.

Jeté In ballet, a travelling jump where the dancer takes off on one leg and lands on the other.

Manon Ballet by British choreographer Kenneth MacMillan from 1974, based on an eighteenth-century French novel. The eponymous leading role of a tragic courtesan is much coveted by female dancers.

Mariinsky Ballet St Petersburg ballet company, based at the Mariinsky Theatre, previously known as the Kirov Ballet and the Imperial Russian Ballet. Founded in the late-eighteenth century, the Mariinsky is one of the world's leading ballet companies, known for its classical purity.

Matthew Bourne's Dorian Gray   A dance version of the Oscar Wilde novel *The Picture of Dorian Gray*, created by Matthew Bourne in 2008.

Mayerling   Ballet by Kenneth MacMillan from 1978, based on the true story of the double suicide of Crown Prince Rudolf of Austria-Hungary and his teenage mistress Mary Vetsera in 1889. The role of Prince Rudolf requires a performance of great emotional depth from its leading man.

Michela Meazza   Italian dancer who performed extensively with Matthew Bourne's New Adventures.

Vaslav Nijinsky   Legendary Russian ballet dancer (1889–1950) famed for his powerful leap and onstage charisma, who performed with Serge Diaghilev's Ballets Russes.

Marianela Nuñez   Argentinian ballerina (*b.* 1982) who is a principal dancer with the Royal Ballet, known for her impeccable technique and soulful performances.

Rudolf Nureyev   Singular Soviet dancer (1938–1993) famous for defecting to the West in 1961 and for his legendary partnership with English ballerina Margot Fonteyn.

Pirouette   A step in ballet where the dancer turns 360 degrees on one leg.

The Place Prize   Biennial choreography prize for UK-based artists.

Sergei Polunin   Ukrainian ballet dancer (*b.* 1989). He was the youngest ever principal dancer at the Royal Ballet, but resigned from the company in 2012. A gifted dancer with a reputation as a rebel.

Prince Rudolf   See *Mayerling*

Prix de Lausanne   Annual international ballet competition held in Switzerland. Previous winners have gone on to stellar careers in dance.

Ivan Putrov   Ukrainian ballet dancer (*b.* 1980). A former principal dancer with the Royal Ballet, Putrov now produces and performs in the Men in Motion series, celebrating the male dancer.

RAD (Royal Academy of Dance)   British dance education organisation, founded in 1920. The RAD exam syllabus is widely used in the UK and internationally.

Rambert   Britain's oldest dance company, founded in 1926 by the Polish dancer Marie Rambert. Originally called Ballet Rambert, the company moved towards contemporary dance in the 1960s. It is now based on London's South Bank.

Relevé   When a dancer rises from their flat foot to the ball of their foot or their pointe.

Jerome Robbins   American choreographer (1918–1998) best known for *West Side Story*, who was also a prolific ballet choreographer.

Rose Adagio   A famously challenging scene in the ballet *Sleeping Beauty* where Princess Aurora must execute a series of difficult balances on pointe.

Royal Ballet School   Full-time ballet school founded in 1926 and based in London, linked to the Royal Ballet company.

Spitfire   All-male quartet choreographed by Matthew Bourne in 1988, which features four dancers in their underwear and is a satire on mail-order catalogue poses and the conventions of classical ballet.

Tour en l'air A step in ballet, usually performed by a man, where the dancer jumps straight up into the air and turns a full circle, landing on the same spot.

Trenches Classic tap-dance step jumping from one foot to the other while leaning forward, like running on the spot with straight arms and legs.

Triple threat Someone who can sing, dance and act.

Turnout Something essential to a ballet dancer, the position of the legs and feet, rotated outwards from the hips.

Vaganova A system of ballet training developed by dancer and teacher Agrippina Vaganova in the early twentieth century. It is the basis of much Russian ballet training.

Mary Vetsera See *Mayerling*

Winter Dreams Ballet from 1991 based on Chekhov's *Three Sisters*, choreographed by Kenneth MacMillan.

Illustrations

Part One: **Jonathan Goddard** in *Fingerprint*, choreography by Richard Alston, The Richard Alston Dance Company, Sadler's Wells, London, 2007. © Nigel Norrington/ArenaPAL

Part Two: **Tamara Rojo** in *Ondine*, choreography by Frederick Ashton, music by Hans Werner Henze, Royal Opera House, London, 2008. © Johan Persson/ArenaPAL

Part Three: **Adam Garcia** in *Saturday Night Fever*, choreography and direction by Arlene Phillips, music, book and lyrics by Nan Knighton and the Bee Gees, London Palladium, 1998. © Michael Ward/ArenaPAL

Part Four: **Darcey Bussell** rehearsing *Le Corsaire* pas de deux, choreography by Marius Petipa, music by Ludwig Minkus and Riccardo Drigo, Royal Opera House, London, 2006. © Johan Persson/ArenaPAL

Part Five: **Steven McRae** in *Connectome*, choreography by Alastair Marriott, music by Arvo Pärt, Royal Opera House, London, 2014. © Bill Cooper/Royal Opera House/ArenaPAL

Part Six: **Kenrick 'H2o' Sandy** in *Pied Piper*, choreography by Kenrick Sandy, music by Michael Asante, Barbican Theatre, London, 2009. © Francis Loney/ArenaPAL

Part Seven: **Seeta Patel**, Mavin Khoo Dance Company, studio portrait. © Eric Richmond/ArenaPAL

Acknowledgements

Enormous thanks to all the dancers and choreographers who gave up their time to be interviewed for this book, as well as their ever-helpful publicists, agents and assistants. All the contributors are artists whose work I have relished watching in my many, many nights at the theatre, and whose conversation I always enjoy. Thanks to Matt Applewhite at Nick Hern Books for his enthusiasm for this project. And thank you to my own dance teacher, Marian Lane, whose classes taught me as much about confidence, commitment and camaraderie as they did about pirouettes and time steps, and were where my enduring love of dance began.

L. W.